The FLAVOR of ITALY

The
FLAVOR
of
ITALY
in Recipes and Pictures

By NARCISSA G. CHAMBERLAIN
and NARCISSE CHAMBERLAIN

Photographs by Samuel Chamberlain

HASTINGS HOUSE, *Publishers,* NEW YORK 22

Introduction

❧

To THOSE for whom Italian food is an adventure and a new experience, the wide variety and the originality of Italian cooking may come as a surprise. English-speaking cooks are too accustomed to thinking that this great cuisine can be summed up by dishes such as spaghetti, pizza, and chicken cacciatore, all lavishly coated with sauces containing generous quantities of tomatoes and garlic. But in fact the cooking of Italy includes an infinite number of delectable recipes, some strong, heavy and rich, as are the classics mentioned above, some as delicate and subtle as any specialty of France or China; some cooked for long periods over a slow fire, many quickly cooked in a few minutes over high heat.

The ingredients are limited only to the extensive variety of products found in this sunny, sea-encompassed land. The types of fish and shellfish greatly outnumber those found on the far longer Atlantic, Gulf, and Pacific coasts. Fruits and vegetables, simple and exotic, thrive in the Italian sunshine; poultry and wild game are used in every province; the rice of Piedmont is basic in the Italian diet, surpassed in popularity only by the ubiquitous pasta with which the Italians have been so inventive that no one has even attempted to list its every known form and style of preparation. Curiously enough, the flavor of the very same egg paste seems to differ with each of its various forms and thicknesses.

Only in its supply of meat does Italy seem less fortunate than some other nations. The climate and geography do not produce large, luxuriant grazing areas, so that good beef is rather scarce and most of the cattle are slaughtered young, producing, however, very fine veal. Lamb and pork are also excellent. With limited meat resources, the Italian chef and housewife have learned with much ingenuity to stretch and vary the supply to flavor soups, sauces, and many aromatic fillings for pasta.

v

Italy's different provinces, which have not been united under one government for very long as history counts time, have retained many of their own customs, local dishes, and even languages. This makes for a certain amount of confusion for the traveler in deciphering restaurant menus. The American is accustomed to a standardization of terms, but he will find in Italy that dining is all the more interesting if he will just dare the unknown. The regional differences quite probably will surprise him. In general, the heavy garlic-flavored dishes are more prevalent in the south where the cooking is done with oil. In the gastronomic centers of the north, he will find a delicate cookery based on butter, many quickly cooked light dishes, and very original sauces such as the famous *pesto*.

The saying goes that a man is what he eats. It is just as true that what he eats is determined by climate and geography. Perhaps the gay, creative, musical, extravert Italian is the natural product of a sunny land abounding in fruits, vegetables and herbs, exotic fish, the aromatic oil of the olive, splendid cheeses, fine rice and wheat. We are fortunate that many of the Italian people and at least some of their cuisine have been transported to other shores. Many Italian-American or Italian-English families continue to cook a larger number of their native dishes than one realizes—with the aid of only a few substitute ingredients and with readily available imported products.

To encourage our readers to follow their example, we have produced this little volume of recipes, illustrated with sunlit and nostalgic pictures of the land of their origin. The recipes, like the pictures, are authentically Italian. They can be made as on Italian soil, with only the barest minimum of changes or substitutions to make them possible in British or American kitchens. They are not adulterated with short-cuts, mixes, fake combinations, or alien products. Many of these dishes have been tasted by the authors in Italy, the recipes for others were contributed by Italian restaurateurs and friends. Therefore, this little book of true Italian cookery offers a savory sample of what the title indicates, the very flavor of Italy.

N.G.C.

Contents

✿

List of Illustrations

ix

Regional Specialties

xiii

The FLAVOR of ITALY

CASTEL SANT'ANGELO *Rome*

Bolognese Meat Sauce

Ragù Bolognese

(Ham, bacon, vegetables, veal, pork, beef, stock, wine, tomato, spices, cream)

In 1 tablespoon of hot butter brown lightly ¼ cup diced ham and ½ cup diced bacon. Add 1 onion, 1 small carrot, and 1 stalk of celery, all finely chopped, and cook until slightly softened. Mix together and add ¼ pound each of veal and pork and ¾ pound of beef, all finely chopped; stir until the red, raw color of the meat disappears. Add ¾ cup of stock and ½ cup white wine, and simmer the mixture until the liquid has almost evaporated. Then add salt and pepper, 3 cloves, a dash of nutmeg, 2 tablespoons of tomato paste, and enough hot water almost to cover the mixture. Simmer the sauce very slowly, covered, for 50 minutes to an hour; it should be very thick. Finally, stir in ½ cup of cream before using. If you add ¼ pound of sliced mushrooms and 2 diced chicken livers 10 minutes before the sauce is finished, it will be even more delicious. Makes between 3 and 4 cups. Use in making green *lasagne bolognese* (*see* Index) or as a sauce for spaghetti, noodles, or homemade *pasta*.

1

FARM COUNTRY   *Umbria*

Lamb Hunter Style

Abbacchio alla Cacciatora

(Spring lamb, lard, rosemary, sage, garlic, wine vinegar, stock, anchovies)

Have 2 pounds of spring lamb cut into 1½-inch cubes, and brown them on all sides in 2 tablespoons of lard. (You may use 1 tablespoon each of butter and olive oil if you prefer.) When the meat is browned, add salt and pepper, ½ teaspoon of rosemary, a pinch of sage, and 1 chopped and mashed clove of garlic. After 2 or 3 minutes, blend in 2 teaspoons of flour and add gradually, stirring well, ½ cup of red-wine vinegar and ¾ cup of hot stock. Cover the pot and simmer the lamb slowly for about 40 minutes, or until it is tender. Chop 4 anchovy fillets and blend them with a little of the hot liquid from the pot. Add this to the lamb, simmer it for 5 minutes more, and sprinkle it with finely minced parsley before serving. Serves four.

SEATED FIGURES — PERUGIA   *Umbria*

Chocolate Ice-Cream Truffles

Tartufo de Cioccolata

(Chocolate ice cream, candied cherries, chocolate fancies, heavy cream)

This dessert takes its name, of course, from the color and shape of the ice-cream balls which resemble giant truffles. Into 1 pint of the best chocolate ice cream mix 4 teaspoons of chopped candied cherries. Scoop the ice cream into 4 round balls, roll each one in chocolate fancies or "jimmies" until thickly coated, and place them on a small cooky sheet. Store them in the refrigerator freezer until hard, and serve with sweetened whipped cream. Serves four.

3

CHAPEL IN THE DOLOMITES   *Trentino-Alto Adige*

Sautéed Artichoke Hearts

Carciofi Fritti

(Frozen artichoke hearts, lemon juice, flour, butter, olive oil)

Allow 1 box of frozen artichoke hearts for three or four. Separate the hearts, and with a sharp knife slice each half artichoke vertically into two or more thin slices. Let them thaw and dry then on paper towels. Sprinkle them with lemon juice, salt, and pepper, let them stand for half an hour, then dust them with flour. Heat together in a skillet 2 tablespoons of butter and 2 or 3 tablespoons of olive oil. When the fat is quite hot, put in the artichoke slices and cook them over moderate heat for 4 or 5 minutes on each side, or until they are well browned and a little crisp. Serve with broiled steaks or roast meats.

THE FORUM							*Rome*

Gnocchi Roman Style
Gnocchi alla Romana
(Cream of wheat or semolina, milk, butter, eggs, Parmesan)

Heat 1 quart of milk, adding a good pinch each of salt and nutmeg. When the milk boils, gradually add 1 cup of cream of wheat, or farina, or Italian *semolina*. Stir well to prevent lumps from forming and cook the mixture for about 10 minutes, or until it is very thick. Cool it a little, then beat in 2 tablespoons of butter, 3 beaten eggs, and ½ cup of grated Parmesan cheese. Spread the *gnocchi* mixture in a ½-inch layer on a board to cool. When it is firm, cut it in squares or circles and arrange these overlapping in rows in a shallow well-buttered baking dish. Sprinkle the *gnocchi* generously with grated Parmesan and melted butter, and brown in a 400° oven. Serves four to six.

GRAVEDONA, ON LAKE COMO   *Lombardy*

Veal Cutlets Milanese
Scaloppine Milanese

(Veal cutlets, milk, flour, egg, bread crumbs, butter, oil, lemon, parsley)

Have very thin slices cut from a leg of veal and flattened by pounding between two pieces of waxed paper. Each piece should be about 5 inches long and less than ¼ inch thick. Soak the slices in a little milk for 1 hour before cooking. Drain and dry the cutlets and season them with salt and pepper. Dip them in flour, in beaten egg, and in fine bread crumbs. For each cutlet, heat about 1 tablespoon each of butter and olive oil in a skillet. Put in the cutlets and turn them almost at once so that too much butter and oil will not be absorbed on one side. Sauté them over low heat for about 5 minutes, then turn them and cook another 5 minutes, or until they are golden brown and crisp. Transfer them to a heated platter, pour the pan juices over them, and garnish each cutlet with a thin slice of lemon sprinkled with minced parsley.

THE PALAZZO DELLA RAGIONE — PADUA   *Veneto Eugenea*

Stuffed Zucchini

Zucchini Ripieni

(Zucchini, onion, garlic, mushrooms, chopped meat, Parmesan, egg, bread crumbs)

Parboil 8 small *zucchini* (Italian squash) for 4 minutes, drain them, and cut them in halves lengthwise. Remove some of the pulp from the centers and reserve it. Sauté 1 small chopped onion in 2 tablespoons of butter until it is soft and golden. Add 1 chopped and mashed clove of garlic and 1½ cups of chopped mushrooms, and cook the mixture slowly for 3 minutes. Remove the pan from the heat and add ¼ pound of chopped beef (or ½ cup of chopped left-over meat of any kind), 2 tablespoons of grated Parmesan, salt and pepper to taste, and the reserved pulp of the *zucchini,* chopped. Mix all together well and stir in 1 lightly beaten egg. Fill the *zucchini* shells with this mixture, and place them in a shallow well-oiled baking dish. Sprinkle them lightly with bread crumbs, then generously with olive oil. Bake them in a 375° oven for about 30 minutes, or until tender and lightly browned. Serve them as they are, or accompanied by tomato sauce. Serves six to eight.

7

CHÂTEAU DE FENIS *Valle d'Aosta*

Chicken Breasts Valdostana

Petti di Pollo alla Valdostana

(Chicken breasts, butter, truffles, Fontina cheese, white wine, stock, brandy)

With a small boning knife, carefully remove the meat from 2 pairs of chicken breasts. This will give you 4 separate pieces or *suprêmes*. Remove the skin and flatten the meat by pounding it between two pieces of waxed paper with the side of a cleaver. Dip the *suprêmes* lightly in flour and cook them slowly for 5 minutes on each side in 2 tablespoons of hot butter. Place them in a broiling pan and season them with salt and pepper. Place on each piece 4 or 5 paper-thin slices of white Italian truffles (or the black variety if you prefer), and over these put a slice of Fontina cheese (Mozzarella or other good mild melting cheeses may be substituted if necessary). To the pan in which the chicken was sautéed add ½ cup of dry white wine, ½ cup of chicken stock, and 1 tablespoon of brandy. Heat this sauce, stirring in all the brown juices in the pan, and simmer it for about 10 minutes. Place the chicken breasts under a hot broiler just long enough to melt the cheese, and serve at once. Stir a small lump of butter into the hot sauce and pass it separately. Serves four.

8

THE FORUM AND THE ARCH OF SEPTIMUS SEVERUS *Rome*

Turkey Breasts Milanese

Petti di Tacchino Milanese

(Turkey breasts, flour, egg, bread crumbs, butter, oil, parsley, lemon)

With a boning knife remove the breasts of an 8- to 10-pound turkey by cutting along the breast bone and then lifting the meat and scraping close to the bones until meat comes away. Remove the skin. Each breast will divide naturally into a large and a small fillet. Cut these into thin slices (you should get at least 8 slices in all), flatten them out by gentle pounding with a cleaver or rolling pin, and trim them to even shapes. Season them with salt and pepper, dip them lightly in flour, then in egg beaten with a few drops of water, and then in fine bread crumbs. Heat butter and oil together, allowing 1 tablespoon of butter and ½ tablespoon of oil for each slice of meat. When the fat is very hot, but not brown, put in the turkey slices and sauté them over moderate heat for 4 to 5 minutes on each side. They should be golden and cooked through without allowing the fat to brown or blacken. Remove them to a hot serving dish, sprinkle them with finely minced parsley, pour any remaining butter over them, and serve with wedges of lemon. Serves four to six.

9

PIAZZA CAVALLI — PIACENZA   *Emilia-Romagna*

Deviled Broiled Chicken
Pollo alla Diavolo

(Chicken, olive oil, sage, red-pepper flakes, white wine)

Have a 2½ -pound chicken split for broiling, rub it inside and out with dried sage and olive oil, and season it with salt and a good dash of crushed red-pepper flakes. Broil the chicken under medium heat for about 15 minutes on each side, or until done, and transfer it to a heated serving platter. Deglaze the juices in the broiling pan with 2 tablespoons of white wine, reheat them briefly on the top of the stove, and pour over the chicken. Serves two.

10

BOBOLI GARDENS — FLORENCE   *Tuscany*

Florentine Beefsteak

Bistecca Fiorentina

(Steak, pepper, olive oil, salt, lemon)

The steaks of Florence are huge and famous because the best beef in Italy is raised in this area of Tuscany. Rub a 1½-inch-thick porterhouse steak (or other tender cut of your choice) on both sides with a little freshly ground pepper and 1 to 2 tablespoons of olive oil. Let it stand for 1 hour before cooking. Broil it over a hot charcoal fire for 6 to 7 minutes on each side, or until the surface is browned but the meat is rare in the center. If you use a gas or electric broiler, preheat it for at least 10 minutes at the highest temperaure. When the steak is done to your taste, salt it and serve it promptly with a little lemon juice squeezed over it and with additional wedges of lemon.

11

LATE AFTERNOON — VERONA   *Veneto Euganea*

Trout in White Wine
Trote in Vino Bianco

(Trout, butter, olive oil, onion, parsley, bay leaf, white wine, croutons)

Heat together 1 tablespoon each of butter and olive oil, and in this sauté briefly 1 chopped onion, adding salt, pepper, a sprig of parsley, and a crumbled bay leaf. When the onion is soft, add 1½ cups of dry white wine and 1 cup of water. Cover the pan and simmer the stock for 5 minutes, then place in it 4 small trout weighing about ½ pound apiece. Cover the pan and poach the fish for 10 minutes; the liquid should not boil during this time but should be kept at almost boiling temperature. Drain the trout, and serve them with a few drops of the cooking liquid and a little browned butter poured over them, and garnished with bread croutons fried in butter. Serves four.

THE MONUMENTS OF PISA   *Tuscany*

Stuffed Flamed Peaches

Pesche Ripiene alla Fiamma

(Peaches, macaroons, almonds, citron, butter, sugar, Marsala, rum)

Peel and halve 6 ripe yellow peaches. Remove the pits and stuff each half with some of the following mixture: Combine ¾ cup of dried and crumbled macaroons, ¼ cup of ground almonds, 2 tablespoons of finely diced citron or candied orange peel, and 2 tablespoons of melted butter. Sprinkle the stuffed peaches with sugar, place them in a shallow baking dish, and pour 1 teaspoon of Marsala or sherry on each half. Bake them in a 375° oven for about 25 minutes, or until just tender. Add a few drops of water to the baking dish, if necessary, to prevent scorching. At the moment of serving, pour 2 tablespoons of warmed rum over the peaches and set it aflame. Serves six to eight.

FARMHOUSE NEAR GRIMALDI   *Calabria*

Fish with Prosciutto

Pesce al Prosciutto

(Small whole fish, lemon juice, olive oil, rosemary, prosciutto, bread crumbs)

Have the heads and backbones removed from 4 small fish—trout, red mullet, mackerel, or any fresh fish of a size suitable to serve one per person. Marinate them for several hours in the following mixture: The juice of 1 lemon, ⅓ cup of olive oil, salt, pepper, and several sprigs of fresh rosemary. Drain the marinade from the fish, place a thin slice of Italian *prosciutto* in the center of each one, and roll them in fine bread crumbs. Place them side by side in a buttered shallow baking dish, pour the marinade over them, and place the dish in a 375° oven for 25 minutes, more or less, until the fish are cooked through and lightly browned. Serves four.

14

HILLSIDE OLIVE GROVE, NEAR BAIARDO   *Liguria*

Duck with Olives
Anitra all'Olivo
(Duck, sage, onion, beef stock, olives)

Rub a 5- to 6-pound duck inside with salt and sage, salt and pepper the outside, and prick the skin at the fattest parts. Cook the duck for 15 minutes in a 550° oven. Pour off all the fat that has been rendered, lower the heat to 450°, and add to the pan 1 chopped onion, 1½ cups of beef stock, the chopped heart of the duck, and ¾ cup (6 ounces) of pitted green Italian olives. Continue roasting the duck, basting often and allowing 15 to 18 minutes per pound of cooking time in all. Half an hour before it is done, add to the pan the duck's liver, cut in six pieces, and a little more stock if needed to make a fairly generous sauce. Carve the duck on a heated platter. Skim as much fat as possible from the pan juices, and serve them in a sauceboat without straining them.

15

THE GRAND CANAL — VENICE   *Veneto Euganea*

Calf's Liver Venetian

Fegato di Vitello alla Veneziana

(Calf's liver, onions, olive oil, sage, parsley)

The secret of this dish is to cut the liver into very, very thin small pieces, about the size of a silver dollar, and to cook them as briefly as possible over a hot fire: Cut ½ pound of young calf's liver into small cutlets as described. Slice 2 medium onions very thinly and brown them in enough hot olive oil to coat well the bottom of an iron skillet. When the onions are lightly browned, add the liver and cook it for about 2 minutes, stirring and tossing to cook it on all sides. Season it with salt, pepper, 3 leaves of fresh sage (or a pinch of dried sage), and 2 teaspoons of finely minced parsley. Heat, stirring, for about another half a minute, and serve at once. Serves two or three.

16

HARBOR AT SAN REMO   *Liguria*

Fillets of Sole Manfredi

Sogliole Manfredi

(Sole, onion, parsley, white wine, egg, bread crumbs, ham, oil, butter, anchovies)

Spread 2 pounds of fillets of sole or flounder evenly in a shallow buttered baking dish. Sprinkle the fish with 1 finely chopped onion, 2 tablespoons of minced parsley, and salt and pepper. Add ¼ cup of dry white wine, cover the dish, and place it in a preheated 400° oven for 4 minutes. Remove the dish, let the fish cool, and drain the juices into a small saucepan and reserve them. Dip the fillets in lightly beaten egg, then in a mixture of 1 cup of fine bread crumbs and 2 tablespoons of finely minced ham. Add a little oil to the baking dish, replace the pieces of fish in it, and over it pour ¼ cup of melted butter. Return the fish to the oven, uncovered, for 20 to 30 minutes, or until it is cooked through and golden. Over low heat, dissolve 3 or 4 minced anchovy fillets in 2 tablespoons of melted butter. Add the reserved fish juices, blend well, and serve this sauce with the fish. Serves six.

17

PIAZZA DÉLLA LIBERTÀ — UDINE   *Friuli-Venezia Giulia*

Assorted Italian Hors-d'Oeuvre

Antipasti I

(Lettuce, salami, prosciutto, tomatoes, peppers, celery, olives, capers, dressing)

On a bed of lettuce leaves on a round platter, arrange the following in rows radiating from the center: Thinly sliced salami, loosely rolled slices of *prosciutto*, sliced ripe tomatoes, and roasted green peppers *(see below)*. Garnish with strips of celery heart or fennel and green and black olives, and sprinkle capers over all. Over the *antipasti* pour several tablespoons of Italian dressing made with three parts olive oil, one part red-wine vinegar or lemon juice, and salt, pepper, and a dash of garlic salt to taste. Serve with *grissini* (bread sticks).

Roasted Green Peppers: Place whole green peppers under a hot broiler and turn them often, until the skins are well browned on all sides. Remove the skins under cold water, dry the peppers well, cut each one into about eight strips, and remove all seeds and fibers. Sprinkle the strips with lemon juice and finely minced garlic, and cover them with olive oil. Marinate them overnight in the refrigerator before serving.

18

POSITANO   *Campania*

Lobster Orègano

Aragosta Oreganata

(Lobsters, herbs, garlic, olive oil, butter, bread crumbs, Parmesan)

Boil two 1½-pound lobsters in salted water for 12 minutes. (This is less than for plain boiled lobster, as these will have further cooking in the oven; too much cooking toughens the meat.) Drain the lobsters well, split them in half lengthwise, and place them shell side down in a baking dish. Melt 1½ tablespoons of butter and add 2 tablespoons of olive oil, 1 tablespoon of chopped parsley, 1 teaspoon of chopped sweet basil, ½ teaspoon of dried orègano, 1 minced and mashed clove of garlic, and a little salt and pepper. Spread this over the lobster tail meat and sprinkle it also with a mixture of 3 tablespoons of bread crumbs and 2 tablespoons of grated Parmesan. Then add a few drops more olive oil, and bake the lobsters in a 400° oven for 15 minutes.

TERRACE AT RAVELLO   *Campania*

Chicken in Cream

Pollo alla Crema

(Chicken, flour, butter, onion, cream, parsley)

Have a young chicken cut into serving pieces and dust them lightly with flour. In a heavy casserole, brown them slowly on all sides in 3 tablespoons of butter, adding also 1 small thinly sliced onion. When the chicken is browned, stir in ¾ cup of cream seasoned with a little salt. Add 1 teaspoon of finely minced parsley, cover the pan, and finish cooking the chicken in a 300° oven, stirring and turning the pieces once or twice. It will be done in half an hour, more or less, depending on the size of the chicken. Serves four.

CA' D'ORO — VENICE   *Veneto*

Aromatic Omelette

Frittata Aromatica

(Eggs, water, Parmesan, fresh mint and basil, butter or olive oil)

The Italian *frittata* differs from the French omelette in that it is not folded but left circular, is browned on both sides, and is more thoroughly cooked:

Beat 6 large eggs with 3 teaspoons of water, 5 tablespoons of grated Parmesan, salt and pepper, and 1 teaspoon each of chopped fresh mint leaves and basil leaves, more or less, according to taste. (Another good combination: orégano, marjoram, and parsley.) Heat 1½ tablespoons of butter (or 2 tablespoons of olive oil) in a skillet, and when it is sizzling pour in the eggs. When they begin to cook, lift the edges here and there to let the liquid run under, and shake the pan back and forth to keep the omelette from sticking. When no more liquid egg remains and the bottom is lightly browned, hold a plate firmly over the top of the skillet with one hand and turn the skillet upside down with the other, leaving the omelette on the plate. Then slip it back into the skillet, cooked side up, and brown the other side briefly. Serve at once. Serves three.

21

FOUNTAIN IN THE MARKETPLACE — L'AQUILA *Abruzzi*

Spaghetti Carbonara
Spaghetti alla Carbonara

(Spaghetti, butter, olive oil, bacon, ham, eggs, Parmesan, Romano, pepper)

Cook 1 pound of spaghetti (*see* Index), and serve it with the following sauce: Heat together, over moderate heat, 2 tablespoons each of butter and olive oil, and add 3 slices of bacon, diced, and ¼ cup of fine julienne strips of ham. Beat 3 eggs with ⅔ cup of grated cheese (half Parmesan and half Romano). When the bacon has barely begun to brown, remove the pan from the fire and stir in the egg mixture very quickly. Blend this sauce immediately with the hot spaghetti, add plenty of freshly ground pepper, and serve at once. The eggs will harden a little in the heat of the fat and the spaghetti. Serves four to six.

22

DOLOMITE LANDSCAPE   *Trentino-Alto Adige*

Chick-Pea Soup
Zuppa de Ceci

(Chick peas, olive oil, onions, green pepper, garlic, seasonings, broth, sausage)

Wash 2 cups of dried chick peas and soak them for 12 hours in water to cover well. Heat ¼ cup of olive oil in a large heavy pot, add 2 onions and 1 green pepper, all chopped, and cook together over low heat for 4 minutes. Add 1 minced clove of garlic, and cook the mixture for 1 minute more. Then add a pinch of red-pepper flakes, 1 bay leaf, the chick peas together with the water in which they were soaked, 4 cups of chicken or beef broth, and salt and pepper to taste. Simmer the soup slowly for about 1½ hours, or until the chick peas are tender. Remove about ½ cup of the peas, force them through a sieve, and return this purée to the soup. Add 12 thin slices of frankfurter sausage, or the equivalent in sliced salami cut in small pieces, and simmer the soup a little longer. Serve with grated Parmesan and toasted Italian bread. Serves six.

SORICO, NEAR LAKE COMO *Lombardy*

Consommé with Poached Eggs

Zuppa alla Pavese

(Italian broth, bread, butter, eggs, Parmesan cheese)

Cut four slices of Italian bread into 3 or 4 pieces and fry them in hot butter until they are brown on both sides. Meanwhile, heat 5 cups of Italian broth (*see* Index) and in it poach 4 eggs, one at a time. As each egg is done, remove is carefully and place it in a hot soup plate. Then strain the hot broth through a fine sieve into each plate. Float the pieces of fried toast around the eggs, sprinkle them with grated Parmesan cheese, and serve at once. Pass more grated cheese with the soup. A meal in itself, for four.

VACATION AT CAPRI   *Campania*

Shirred Eggs with Anchovies

Uova al Piatto con Acciughe

(Eggs, butter, pepper, anchovies, Mozzarella)

Butter 4 shirred-egg dishes, break an egg into each one, season them with a little pepper, and place on each egg 1 anchovy fillet and a thin slice of Mozzarella cheese. Put the dishes in a 400° oven and cook the eggs 10 minutes, or until the whites are set, the yolks are still soft, and the cheese is melted. Meanwhile, heat together 4 tablespoons butter and 4 minced anchovy fillets (or the equivalent in anchovy paste) until the anchovies are dissolved and blended with the butter. Pour this sauce over the eggs and serve at once. Serves four.

25

SORRENTO   *Campania*

Onions with Mushrooms

Cipolle ai Funghi

(Onions, olive oil, mushrooms, garlic, parsley)

Cover 1½ pounds of medium white boiling onions, unpeeled, with cold water. Bring the water to a boil, then cook the onions for 12 minutes. Peel them, and place them in a casserole with ½ cup of olive oil, ¾ pound of quartered mushroom caps, 2 chopped and mashed cloves of garlic, 1 tablespoon of minced parsley, and salt and pepper. Cover the casserole and bake the onions in a 300° oven for 1 hour, or until they are tender. Remove the cover for the last 20 minutes to reduce the juices if necessary. Serves four.

VILLAGE CHURCH — SAN VITO   *Lombardy*

Braised Beef Lombardy

Manzo Stufato alla Lombarda

(Rump of beef, nutmeg, red wine, garlic, bacon, vegetables, parsley, lemon peel)

Choose a 3-pound piece of rump or round of beef, free of fat. Rub it with salt, pepper, and a little grated nutmeg, and marinate it for 5 hours in 1 cup of red wine with 1 cut clove of garlic. Drain and dry the beef and rub it with flour. Heat 1 tablespoon of oil and 3 tablespoons of diced bacon in a heavy pot. When the bacon has given off most of its fat, but before it browns, add the beef and brown it evenly on all sides. Then add the marinade, discarding the garlic, and add 1 carrot, 1 onion, and 1 stalk of celery, all cut in pieces, a sprig of parsley, a strip of lemon peel, salt and pepper, and about ¾ cup of water or stock, or enough to come half way up the piece of meat. Cover the pot and simmer the beef over the lowest possible heat for about 2 or 3 hours, or until it is tender. Serves six or more.

27

NAPLES, OLD AND NEW   *Campania*

Green Sauce
Salsa Verde

(Parsley, capers, pickle, garlic, bread crumbs, salt, pepper, sugar, oil, vinegar)

Combine ¾ cup of finely minced parsley, 1½ tablespoons of Italian salted capers (first washed and dried), 1½ tablespoons of chopped sour cucumber pickle, and about ¼ clove of garlic, chopped and mashed. Add a slice of bread without the crust, crumbled. Mash these all well together in a mortar or wooden bowl, and force the mixture through a coarse sieve. Add freshly ground pepper, a very moderate amount of salt, and a pinch of sugar. Stir in gradually about ¼ cup of olive oil and about ⅜ cup of wine vinegar. The latter depends on your taste; the sauce should be quite tart, but remember the capers and pickle have contributed their flavor. This sauce is delicious with poached fish, with cold meats, or with boiled meats such as *bollito* (*see* Index).

THE BAPTISTRY — PISA   *Tuscany*

Strawberry Whipped-Cream Sauce
Crema Montata alla Fragole
(Strawberries, powdered sugar, Maraschino liqueur, cream)

Mash enough fresh strawberries through a fine sieve to make ¼ cup of purée. Mix it well with 3 tablespoons of powdered sugar and 1 tablespoon of Maraschino liqueur. Whip 1 cup of chilled heavy cream until it is fluffy, and mix in the strawberry purée. Serve at once with meringues, sponge cake, or angel cake. Serves four. You may also use frozen strawberries for this: Drain off some of the juice before making the purée and do not add sugar.

29

AMALFI   *Campania*

Beef Tenderloin with Madeira

Filetto al Madera

(Beef tenderloin, butter, bacon, onion, beef stock, Madeira)

Heat 2 teaspoons of butter in a heavy skillet, add 1½ tablespoons of diced bacon, and brown the bacon slowly. When it begins to take on color, add 1 small sliced onion; when the onion is golden, remove both onion and bacon and discard them. In the remain fat, brown 4 one-inch-thick slices of tenderloin of beef over high heat for 2 minutes on each side. Season them with salt and pepper, and add 1½ tablespoons of melted butter, ¼ cup of hot beef stock, and ¼ cup of Madeira. Continue cooking over moderate heat for another 2 minutes on each side. Serve the tenderloins at once, with the pan juices poured over them.

FAMILY GROUP — AVETRANA   *Basilicata*

Sautéed Fish with Tomato Sauce
Pesce alla Luciana

(Fish, butter, olive oil, garlic, parsley, tomatoes, clams)

For this dish you may use 1½ pounds of any good firm fish—a slice, or fillets, or small whole fish. Dip the fish in seasoned flour. Heat together 1 tablespoon of butter and 2 tablespoons of olive oil, and sauté the fish in this, browning it on both sides. Add 1 minced clove of garlic, 1 teaspoon of minced parsley, and 1 cup of canned Italian tomatoes. Then cook the fish, covered, over low heat for about 10 minutes. Add 8 or 10 shucked clams, and cook for 3 more minutes. Sprinkle with more minced parsley before serving. Serves three or four.

31

PEBBLE BEACH — CAMOGLI

Liguria

Fish in Paper Cases

Triglie in Cartoccio

(Mullet or other fish, prosciutto, mushrooms, parsley, olive oil)

The original recipe calls for red mullet, but other small fish may be substituted, such as lake trout, butterfish, small mackerel, or whatever your local specialty may be.

For each small fish prepare a rectangle of doubled heavy parchment paper or aluminum foil. Place the fish in the center, and cover it with a mixture of 1 teaspoon of chopped *prosciutto* or ham, 1 teaspoon of chopped mushrooms, ½ teaspoon of chopped parsley, and salt and pepper. Pour 2 teaspoons of olive oil on each fish, wrap the paper or foil around them, and fold the edges securely to seal the packets hermetically. No steam or juice should escape during the cooking. Place the fish side by side in a shallow baking dish, and bake them in a 375° oven for about 30 minutes, depending on their size. Serve them in their papers, which are opened on the plate by each guest to preserve the juices inside.

CASTELLO SCALIGERO — SIRMIONE   *Lombardy*

Rice with Egg and Lemon

Riso all'Uovo e Limone

(Rice, eggs, lemon juice, Parmesan)

Cook 2 cups of rice in 3 quarts of rapidly boiling salted water for about 15 minutes, or until tender. Drain it well and return it to the pot. Meanwhile, beat together well 3 eggs, the juice of 1 lemon, and ¾ cup of grated Parmesan cheese. Stir this mixture into the hot rice, over a low fire, and serve immediately. Serves six.

UMBRELLA PINES — RAVELLO   *Campania*

Salt Cod with Tomato Sauce

Baccalà al Pomodoro

(Salt cod, flour, olive oil, garlic, tomatoes, parsley)

Soak 2 pounds of salt-cod fillets in water for 24 hours (or according to directions on the package), then drain them and rinse them in fresh water. Cut the fillets into 3-inch pieces and dry them. Dip the pieces in flour, sauté them in hot olive oil until they are golden brown on each side, and place them in a shallow baking dish. To the oil left in the pan, add enough fresh olive oil to make about 4 tablespoons in all. In this brown 2 cut cloves of garlic, then remove the garlic, and add 2 pounds of tomatoes, peeled and coarsely chopped, and salt and pepper to taste. Heat the mixture until it simmers, then pour it over the fish. Bake the fish in a 375° oven for about 30 minutes, or until it is tender and the sauce is thickened. Sprinkle with minced parsley before serving. Serves four.

34

SKYLINE OF FLORENCE   *Tuscany*

Roast Loin of Pork with Chestnuts

Lombo di Maiale con Castagne

(Pork loin, garlic, rosemary, cloves, Italian chestnuts)

Use a 4-pound roast from the center of the loin. Insert 3 cut cloves of garlic here and there in the meat, score the fat with shallow cuts, rub these with salt, pepper, and ½ teaspoon of rosemary, and stick 4 or 5 cloves into the fat. Add a little hot water to the pan, and roast the pork, fat side up, in a 350° oven for about 45 minutes per pound. Twenty minutes before the roast is done, surround it with Italian chestnuts prepared as follows:

Cut a gash in the flat sides of the shells of 1½ pounds of Italian chestnuts. In an iron skillet, over a hot fire, stir them for about 5 minutes in 1 tablespoon of oil. Cool and peel them, then boil them gently in hot salted water or stock to cover for about 15 minutes. Do not let them get soft enough to break up. Drain the chestnuts and remove any remaining skin. Put them in the roasting pan with the pork, and baste them with the pan juices. When the pork is done, serve it sliced on a hot platter, surrounded by the chestnuts. Serves eight.

35

VIA APPIA ANTICA — ROME   *Latium*

Roman Consommé

Straciatella

(Chicken broth, eggs, parsley, Parmesan)

Beat 3 eggs well, add 2 tablespoons of finely minced parsley and 3 tablespoons of grated Parmesan (or 2 tablespoons of grated Romano, which is stronger), and mix well. Heat 6 cups of rich clear chicken broth and, just before it reaches the boiling point, gradually add the egg mixture, stirring very slowly all the while. Stir the soup just until the eggs set into strands, and serve at once. Serves six.

PIAZZA SAN PETRO   *Rome*

Veal Cutlets Roman Style
Saltimbocca alla Romana

(Veal cutlets, sage, prosciutto, butter, white wine)

Have cutlets cut as thin as possible from a leg of veal and pounded between two pieces of waxed paper to flatten them; they should be less than ¼ inch thick. Place a leaf of fresh sage on each one, season them with salt and pepper, and cover each one with a thin slice of *prosciutto* or ham. Fasten veal and ham together by taking a "stitch" with a wooden toothpick. For 8 cutlets melt 4 to 5 tablespoons of butter in a large skillet. Arrange the cutlets in one layer in the skillet, and sauté them for 6 minutes on the veal side and 4 minutes on the ham side. Transfer the *saltimbocca* to a hot platter. Stir ½ cup of dry white wine into the pan juices, simmer this sauce for a minute or two, and spoon it over the meat. Serves four.

INNER HARBOR — CESENATICO   *Emilia-Romagna*

Shrimp Cacciatora

Gamberetti alla Cacciatora

(Shrimp, butter, oil, onion, garlic, tomatoes, green pepper, mushrooms, wine)

In a saucepan heat together 1 tablespoon of butter and 2 tablespoons of olive oil. Add 1 chopped onion and 1 clove of garlic, cut in two. When the onion is soft and pale gold, add 2 cups of canned Italian plum tomatoes and 1 green pepper, cleaned and cut into 8 or 10 slices. Cook this sauce for 15 minutes, then add ½ pound of sliced fresh mushrooms and ½ cup of dry white wine. Continue cooking, covered, for about 20 minutes, or until the sauce is of a good consistency. Remove the pieces of garlic, and add 1 pound of raw shrimp, shelled and deveined. Simmer the shrimp in the sauce for 15 minutes, or until done. Arrange a ring of fluffy boiled rice on a serving dish, and pour the shrimp with their sauce into the center. Serves three or four.

THE CAMPIDOGLIO   *Rome*

Risotto Milanese

Risotto alla Milanese

(Rice, butter, olive oil, onion, garlic, chicken stock, saffron, Madeira, Parmesan)

The principle of cooking Italian *risotto* is first to cook the raw rice very slightly in fat, and then to add stock in two or more operations, allowing the rice to absorb the liquid gradually until done. It should be tender but rather dry. One cup of rice absorbs about 3½ cups of liquid. Stir the *risotto* as little as possible throughout, and then only with a large two-pronged fork.

In a heavy pan heat together 2 tablespoons each of butter and olive oil. Stir in 1 cup of rice and, when it is a pale golden color, add 1 chopped onion and 1 chopped and mashed clove of garlic. Stir over the heat for about 2 minutes, then add 1 cup of hot chicken stock. Cook the rice over low heat, covered, for about 15 minutes, or until the liquid is absorbed. Blend ½ teaspoon of saffron with 3 tablespoons of Madeira, and add this to the rice. Add 2½ cups of hot chicken stock, stir the rice just once, cover again, and continue cooking very slowly until all the liquid is absorbed. Then add ½ cup of grated Parmesan and 2 teaspoons of butter, stir all together lightly, and serve the *risotto* at once. Serves four.

VILLAGE FOUNTAIN — VETRALLA   *Latium*

Egg Salad

Insalata di Uova

(Eggs, olive oil, vinegar, scallions, celery, parsley)

Slice 4 hard-boiled eggs and arrange them prettily on a small platter. Combine 3 tablespoons of olive oil and 1 tablespoon of wine vinegar, add salt and pepper to taste, and mix together well. Stir in 1½ tablespoons of chopped young green scallions, 2 tablespoons of finely diced celery, and 1 teaspoon of minced parsley. Pour this dressing over the eggs and serve as a first-course *antipasto*. Serves four.

ITALIAN VILLA, NEAR SPELLO   *Umbria*

Hot Wine Custard
Zabaione

(Eggs, sugar, Marsala, strawberries, brandy)

For each person allow 2 egg yolks, 2 tablespoons of fine granulated sugar, and 4 tablespoons of Marsala, and add 1 egg white for each 4 yolks. In the top of a double boiler beat well together the yolks, whites, and sugar until the mixture is thick and creamy. Add the Marsala, place the pan over very slowly simmering water, and beat the custard well with a whisk or rotary beater until it is hot, thick, and fluffy. Never allow it to boil, or it will separate. Serve immediately, in warmed stem glasses. If you wish, you may place in the bottoms of the glasses a few strawberries soaked with a little brandy and sugar. Spoon the *zabaione* over the berries and serve at once.

41

DOLOMITE CHAPEL — VAL DI FASSA   *Trentino-Alto Adige*

Eggplant Parmesan
Melanzana Parmigiana
(Eggplant, olive oil, tomato sauce, Parmesan, Mozzarella)

Peel a large eggplant and cut it in slices not over ⅓ inch thick. Salt the slices, let them stand 1 hour, then drain off the liquid. Dip each slice in flour and sauté them slowly in olive oil until they are brown on each side; drain the slices on absorbent paper. In the bottom of a shallow oiled baking dish place half the eggplant slices in one layer. Season them with a little salt and pepper, cover them with prepared tomato sauce, and on this sprinkle a good quantity of grated Parmesan, then add a layer of sliced Mozzarella cheese. Add the rest of the eggplant and repeat the operation as before, ending with the slices of Mozzarella. Sprinkle olive oil on the surface and place the dish in a 350° oven for about 30 minutes. Brown the surface under the broiler at the end if desired.

42

ASCOLI PICENO   *Marche*

Vegetable Soup Rossi
Minestrone Rossi

(Dried beans, cabbage, carrots, turnips, onion, salt pork, tomato, celery, garlic)

Soak 1 cup of dried white beans overnight. Drain them and put them in a kettle with 3 quarts of fresh water and 2 teaspoons of salt. Simmer them very slowly for 1 hour, than add 1 small cabbage, sliced, 2 carrots and 2 white turnips, all diced, and other fresh green vegetables if desired. Cook the vegetables all together for another hour.

Meanwhile, in another pan, sauté 1 sliced onion and 1 tablespoon of diced salt pork in 1 tablespoon each of butter and olive oil. When the onion is soft and lightly browned, add 1 large peeled and coarsely chopped tomato, 1 chopped celery stalk with its leaves, 1 tablespoon of chopped parsley, 1 minced clove of garlic, and salt and pepper to taste. Cook the mixture slowly for 20 minutes, stirring often. One half hour before the soup is done, add the sautéed mixture to it, together with 1 cup of broken-up thin spaghetti. Serve the *minestrone* in large soup bowls with grated Parmesan to sprinkle on top. Serves eight.

CHÂTEAU DE ST. PIERRE   *Valle d'Aosta*

Melon and Prosciutto

Antipasto di Melone e Prosciutto

(Melon, or fresh figs, prosciutto, black pepper)

Three large, very thin slices of *prosciutto* are about right for each serving. Cut a generous section of chilled ripe melon for each person (a Persian or Cranshaw melon, or a large cantaloupe, will serve six). Slice the melon sections into thin crescents, remove the rind, and arrange these in overlapping rows on each plate with the *prosciutto*, rolled loosely, beside them. Black pepper from the pepper mill is the usual seasoning. When ripe figs are in season, they make a fine substitute for the melon; allow 2 or 3 per person.

THE DUCAL PALACE — URBINO

Guinea Fowl in Casserole

Gallina di Faraone in Casseruola

(Guinea fowl, juniper berries, stock, brandy, grapes, white wine, butter, Madeira)

Clean and wipe a 2½-pound guinea fowl (a pheasant is equally good prepared this way), season it inside and out with salt and pepper, and place 8 or 10 crushed juniper berries in the cavity. In a heavy casserole, on top of the stove, melt 1 tablespoon of butter, and in it brown the bird evenly on all sides. Add 2 tablespoons of stock and 1 tablespoon of brandy, cover, and finish cooking the bird in a 300° oven. This will take 45 minutes to 1 hour in all. Add a little stock if necessary or, on the contrary, remove the cover if too much liquid forms during the cooking.

Meanwhile soak 2 dozen seedless grapes (or Muscats with the seeds removed) in ¼ cup of white wine. Fifteen minutes before the guinea fowl is done, remove it temporarily to a plate. Add 1 teaspoon of butter to the juices in the casserole, stir in the white wine and grapes, replace the bird, and baste it with the sauce. Flame 1 tablespoon of brandy over it, add 1 tablespoon of Madeira, and finish cooking the bird in the oven, uncovered, basting it once or twice. A purée of chestnuts is a good accompaniment. Serves four.

VESUVIUS AND THE BAY OF NAPLES *Campania*

Neapolitan Salad
Insalata alla Napoletana

(Cauliflower, dressing, anchovies, capers, black olives, lettuce, pimientos)

Wash a large cauliflower and divide it into flowerets. Drop these into boiling salted water and cook them for 7 minutes. Drain them, rinse them in cold water, and chill them in the refrigerator. Combine ½ teaspoon of salt, ¼ teaspoon of freshly ground pepper, 2 tablespoons of wine vinegar, 5 tablespoons of olive oil, 1 tablespoon of capers, 1 teaspoon of minced parsley, and a dozen pitted and chopped Italian black olives. Mix this dressing and the cauliflower carefully together, and arrange the salad on a bed of lettuce or heart of escarole leaves. Decorate with strips of sweet red pimientos. Serves six.

TYPICAL "TRULLI" — ALBEROBELLA   *Apulia*

Buttered Noodles
Tagliatelle al Burro

(Egg noodles, butter, cream, Parmesan)

Tagliatelle, or *fettuccine,* which are practically the same thing, are narrow egg noodles made of the same paste as many other members of the large Italian *pasta* family. Their names, such as *lasagne, ravioli, cannelloni, agnolotti,* etc., are too numerous to list; they indicate the various sizes and forms into which the paste is cut and shaped.

Boil 1 pound of egg noodles in a generous quantity of salted water until they are done but not too soft. Drain them thoroughly and pour them into a heated serving bowl. Add 6 tablespoons of soft sweet butter, cut in small pieces, 1 tablespoon of heavy cream, and a generous dusting of grated Parmesan. Toss quickly and thoroughly all together, and serve at once. This is one of the simplest and yet most delicious of the many Italian *pasta* dishes. Serves four to six.

47

BERNINI FOUNTAIN   *Rome*

Baked Apples in Red Wine

Mele in Vino Rosso

(Apples, sugar, nutmeg, cloves, cinnamon, red wine)

Core 4 firm baking apples but do not pierce them completely through the bottoms. Peel the tops a little less than half way down, leaving the rest of the skin intact. Put the apples, peeled halves up, in a deep baking dish the right size to hold them closely together. Measure out 1 cup of sugar, fill the centers with some of it, and grate a dash of nutmeg over each apple. Add to the dish 2 whole cloves, a very small piece of cinnamon stick, 2 cups of red wine, and 1 cup of water, or enough to almost half cover the apples. Add the remaining sugar, coating the tops of the apples generously and putting the rest into the wine. Bake in a moderately hot oven (385°) for 30 to 40 minutes, or until the apples are just soft. Serve hot or cold. Serves four.

48

PERDENONE
Friuli-Venezia Giulia

Italian Rice with Chicken Livers

Risotto alla Finanziera

(Italian rice, onion, chicken livers, lemon, mushrooms, stock, Marsala, Parmesan)

Make a simple Italian rice (*risotto*; *see* Index) and serve it with the following sauce added: Sauté 1 finely chopped onion slowly in 3 tablespoons of hot butter until it is pale gold. Add 4 chicken livers, each cut into 4 pieces, together with a small strip of lemon peel and 4 sliced mushrooms. Season the mixture with salt and pepper, cook it for 2 or 3 minutes, stirring once or twice, and add 2 tablespoons each of stock and dry Marsala or Madeira. Cover the saucepan and simmer the sauce for about 10 minutes. Then remove the piece of lemon peel, add the sauce to the prepared *risotto*, and place it in a hot serving dish. Sprinkle ¼ cup of grated Parmesan cheese over the top and serve at once. Serves four.

49

HADRIAN'S VILLA — TIVOLI   *Latium*

Artichokes and Peas
Carciofi con Piselli

(Artichoke hearts, lemon, butter, olive oil, prosciutto, onion, peas, stock)

Thaw 1 package of sliced frozen young artichoke hearts. Dry the slices, sprinkle them with lemon juice, and let them stand for 1 hour. In a saucepan heat together 3 tablespoons of butter, 2 tablespoons of olive oil, and 4 tablespoons of diced *prosciutto* or lean bacon. Add half a small onion, chopped, and sauté it slowly until soft but not brown. Add the artichoke hearts, about 2 cups of small fresh peas (or frozen small peas), salt and pepper, a pinch of sugar, and ½ cup of chicken stock. Cover the saucepan and simmer the vegetables slowly for about 20 minutes, or until they are tender. Serves four.

IMPRUNETA   *Tuscany*

Beans Tuscany

Fagioli all'Uccelletto

(Dried white beans, garlic, sage, olive oil, tomatoes)

Soak 1½ cups of dried white beans in water overnight. Drain them and place them in a saucepan with 1 quart of water, 2 chopped cloves of garlic, ½ teaspoon of sage, 3 tablespoons of olive oil, and 2 peeled, seeded, and coarsely chopped tomatoes. Cover the pan and simmer the beans very slowly for about 2 hours, or until they are tender but not broken and the sauce is reduced and thick. Season the beans with salt and pepper before serving. Serves four.

TRULLI FARMHOUSE, NEAR LOCOROTONDO   *Apulia*

Shirred Eggs Parmesan

Uova alla Parmigiana

(Eggs, olive oil, prosciutto, Parmesan, butter)

Grease 4 shirred-egg dishes with a little olive oil and break an egg into each one. Sprinkle the eggs with a little salt. Cut 2 thin slices of *prosciutto* or ham into fine slivers and sprinkle these over the eggs. Cover the surface of each egg with about ½ tablespoon of grated Parmesan and pour over each one ½ tablespoon of melted butter. Place the dishes in a 400° oven for 10 minutes, or until the whites are set, the yolks are still soft, and the cheese is lightly browned. Serves four.

WINE BARRELS — VITERBO   *Latium*

Braised Beef with Red Wine
Stufato di Manzo al Vino Rosso

(Round of beef, nutmeg, herbs, garlic, red wine, olive oil, bacon, onion, stock)

Rub a 2½-pound piece of round of beef with salt, pepper, and a dash of grated nutmeg. Put it in a bowl with 1 bay leaf, a pinch of orégano, 1 cut clove of garlic, and 1 cup of red wine. Cover the bowl and let the beef marinate for 4 hours, turning it once. Remove the meat, wipe it with paper towels, and reserve the marinade. In a heavy casserole heat together 1 tablespoon of olive oil and 1 slice of bacon. When the bacon is crisp, discard it. Dust the meat lightly with flour and, over moderate heat, brown it a little on all sides in the fat. Add 1 thinly sliced onion and cook it until it is transparent. Strain the marinade, add it to the casserole, cover closely, and put it in a 275° oven for about 3 hours, or until the beef is tender. Add a little hot stock during the cooking if the sauce reduces too much. Serves four to six.

53

THE FORUM — POMPEII   *Campania*

Stuffed Roast Chicken

Pollo Ripieno Arrosto

(Chicken, olive oil, butter, onion, ham, bread crumbs, Parmesan, stock)

Prepare the following stuffing for a 4- to 5-pound chicken: Heat together 2 tablespoons of olive oil and 3 tablespoons of butter, and in this sauté 1 chopped onion until it is soft and golden. Add the chopped liver and heart of the chicken, ½ cup of minced ham, and 1½ cups of coarse stale bread crumbs. Stir all together over moderate heat until the crumbs are lightly browned. Then add salt and pepper, ¼ cup of grated Parmesan cheese, and ½ cup of stock. Heat and stir together briefly, then cool completely before stuffing the chicken. Roast the bird in the usual way, first rubbing it with butter, salt, and pepper, and allowing about 20 minutes per pound in a 300° oven.

BASILICA OF SAN FRANCESCO — ASSISI   *Umbria*

Chicken Cacciatora
Pollo alla Cacciatora

(Chicken, olive oil, butter, onion, garlic, basil, parsley, tomatoes, red wine)

Cut a 4-pound chicken into serving pieces and, in a heavy pot, brown them on all sides in a mixture of 2 tablespoons of olive oil and 1 tablespoon of butter. Remove the chicken and keep it warm. To the fat in the pot add 1 large sliced onion and 1 clove of garlic, cut in two, and cook them slowly until the onion is soft. Add salt and pepper, 4 or 5 leaves of fresh basil (or a pinch of dried basil), and 1 teaspoon of chopped parsley, and cook and stir the mixture for one or two minutes more. Drain most of the liquid from a 1-pint can of Italian plum tomatoes and reserve it. Add the pulp of the tomatoes to the pot, together with ½ cup of red wine. Add the pieces of chicken to this sauce and simmer it, covered, for about 30 minutes, or until it is tender. The sauce should be rather thick, but if it dries out too much add some of the reserved tomato juice as it cooks. Serves four.

THE BEACH AT BOGLIASCO   *Liguria*

Strawberry Ice

Gelato di Fragole

(Strawberries, water, sugar)

Over moderate heat boil together 2 cups of water and 1¼ cups of granulated sugar for 15 minutes. Meanwhile, mash and strain through a colander 1 pint of sweet ripe strawberries. Add the sugar syrup to the strawberries and force the mixture through a fine strainer. This ice may be frozen in a hand-turned freezer, in an automatic electric one, or in a deep tray in the refrigerator. In the latter case, it is necessary to beat the ice several times as it freezes with a hand or electric rotary beater. Serves four.

RUINS OF THE ANCIENT THEATER — TAORMINA *Sicily*

Baked Artichokes Sicilian

Carciofi alla Siciliana

(Artichokes, bread crumbs, Parmesan, parsley, garlic, olive oil)

Cut the stems from 6 medium artichokes and trim ½ inch from the tip of each leaf. Parboil the artichokes for 7 minutes in salted water and drain them well. Spread the leaves apart and at the base of each leaf insert some of the following stuffing: 1¼ cups of bread crumbs, 1¼ cups of grated Parmesan, ¾ cup of finely chopped parsley, and salt and pepper to taste. Place a piece of garlic in the center of each artichoke. Put the artichokes in a heavy casserole, pour in water to a depth of about ½ inch, and pour 1 tablespoon of olive oil on each one. Cover the casserole and cook the artichokes in a 300° oven for about 1 hour, or until a leaf pulls away with ease. Remove the garlic before serving. Serves six.

FAÇADE OF THE CATHEDRAL — MILAN   *Lombardy*

Roast Squab

Piccioncini Arrosti

(Squab, rosemary, bacon)

Allow 1 squab per person. Wash and dry them and rub the cavities with salt, pepper, and a pinch of rosemary. Tie strips of bacon over the breast of each bird, truss them, and place them on the spit of an electric rotisserie. Roast them for about 30 minutes, or until brown and tender, and remove the bacon strips before serving. Serve with Peas and *Prosciutto* (*see* Index).

BELLAGIO, ON THE COMO   *Lombardy*

Stuffed Turkey Lombardy
Tacchino Ripieno alla Lombarda

(Turkey, veal, sausage, chestnuts, apple, bacon, onion, herbs, Parmesan, eggs)

For a 10-pound turkey make the following stuffing: Combine ½ pound of chopped veal or lean beef; ½ pound sweet Italian sausage, skinned and chopped; 15 Italian chestnuts, peeled, boiled, and crumbled; 1 firm apple, peeled and diced; 3 slices of bacon, diced; 1 onion, chopped and cooked in butter until soft; and the liver and giblets of the bird, boiled and chopped. Mix these ingredients together well and add ½ teaspoon salt, ⅛ teaspoon each of pepper and grated nutmeg, ½ cup of grated Parmesan, ¼ teaspoon of dried sage, a pinch of thyme, and 2 eggs. Mix all together thoroughly, stuff the turkey loosely, sew it up, and place it in a roasting pan. Sprinkle it with a little salt and pepper and ¼ teaspoon of rosemary, and rub it with butter. Roast it in a 325° oven, allowing 15 minutes per pound, and basting often. Add ¾ cup of white wine to the pan, a little at a time, during the last hour. Serve the pan juices separately as a sauce for the turkey.

MONT BLANC, FROM COURMAYEUR   *Valle d'Aosta*

Veal Chops with Cheese
Costelette di Vitello con Formaggio
(Veal chops, Fontina cheese, flour, egg, bread crumbs, butter, lemon)

Trim all fat and gristle from 4 half-inch-thick veal chops. Cut into the side of each one to form a horizontal pocket. In this insert a slice of Fontina cheese. Season the chops with salt and pepper, and dip them in flour, beaten egg, and bread crumbs. Sauté them, over medium heat, in 6 tablespoons of hot butter for 10 minutes on each side. Remove them to a hot platter, pour the remaining pan juices over them, and serve with wedges of lemon. Serves four.

CHURCH OF SAN MICHELE — LUCCA   *Tuscany*

Leghorn Fish Stew

Cacciucco Livornese

(Lobster, squid, scallops, fish, oil, garlic, herbs, white wine, tomato paste)

The Italians make many types of fish soup *(zuppa di pesce)*, though "stew" is perhaps a more descriptive term. Those of Leghorn in Tuscany are particularly famous. You will need 1 small live lobster (cut it in sections and discard the head), enough squid (optional) to make 1 cup of skinned, cleaned, and sliced meat, 1 cup of diced scallops, and 1½ pounds of firm white fish such as haddock and halibut, cut in 1½-inch sections. In ½ cup of olive oil heat until softened 1 or 2 minced cloves of garlic with 2 teaspoons of minced parsley and 2 or 3 leaves of sage. Add the pieces of lobster with their shells, and the squid, and season with salt, pepper, and a good dash of crushed red-pepper flakes. Cover the pot and cook the fish over low heat, stirring occasionally, for 10 minutes. Then add ½ cup of dry white wine and continue cooking until this is half evaporated. Dissolve 2 tablespoons of tomato paste in 3 cups of hot water; add this and the rest of the fish to the stew, and simmer it for 20 minutes more. Taste for seasoning, and serve with Italian bread which has been rubbed with garlic and toasted and buttered. Serves six.

61

CANAL BY THE SCUOLA DI SAN MARCO — VENICE　　*Veneto Euganea*

Grilled Shrimp with Oil and Lemon

Scampi alla Griglia con Olio e Limone

(Shrimp, olive oil, parsley, butter, lemon juice)

Split 2 pounds of jumbo shrimp lengthwise down the centers, without separating the halves completely and without cutting through the back of the shell. Thread each one on a small skewer or a wooden toothpick, pinning them from the inside out, and back in again, to hold them flat. Dip the shrimp in a mixture of ½ cup of olive oil, 2 tablespoons of minced parsley, and a pinch of salt. Broil them under high heat for about 2 minutes on each side, then place them shell side down in a warm baking dish. Over them sprinkle ¼ cup of melted butter combined with the juice of 1 large lemon, and put them in a 400° oven for about 5 minutes to finish cooking. Serves six.

ISOLA BELLA — LAKE MAGGIORE   *Piedmont*

Frozen Chestnut Pudding
Plombière alla Torinese

(Eggs, sugar, milk, chestnut purée, maraschino liqueur, heavy cream)

In the top of a double boiler beat together well 3 eggs and ¼ cup of sugar. Add gradually 1¾ cups of scalded milk, stirring constantly. Place the pan over slowly simmering water, and cook the custard, stirring often, for 6 to 8 minutes, or until it thickens. Mix 3 tablespoons of maraschino liqueur into 1½ cups of canned *crème de· marrons* (sweetened and vanilla-flavored chestnut purée), then add the custard and mix well. Freeze the pudding in a deep ice tray, stirring it from time to time. When it is almost but not quite frozen hard, whip ½ cup of heavy cream and stir this into the pudding, but not too thoroughly. Freeze the pudding a brief while longer, and serve somewhat soft and not completely frozen. Serves eight.

63

SANTUARIO DELLA SANTA CASA — LORETO *Marche*

Marinated Shrimp

Gamberetti con Olio e Limone

(Shrimp, seasonings, lemon juice, olive oil)

For 1 pound of shrimp, boil together for 5 minutes 1 quart of water, 1 table-spoon of vinegar, 1 small sliced onion, a few celery leaves, a pinch of salt, and several crushed peppercorns. Add the shrimp, bring the liquid to a boil, and simmer them for 5 to 8 minutes, depending on their size. Drain, peel, and devein them. Place the shrimp in a bowl with 1½ tablespoons of lemon juice, 4½ table-spoons of olive oil, and salt and pepper, and marinate them in the refrigerator for several hours. Serve as a first-course *antipasto,* with fresh Italian bread and a chilled dry white wine. Serves four.

LAKE GARDA   *Piedmont*

Peas with Prosciutto

Piselli al Prosciutto

(Peas, prosciutto, olive oil, onion, chicken stock, parsley)

In a saucepan put ¼ cup olive oil, 2 cups small tender peas (the smaller frozen peas are good for this dish), ½ small onion, finely minced, ¼ cup of *prosciutto* or other ham, cut in very thin julienne strips, ½ cup of chicken stock, and salt and pepper. When the liquid begins to boil, cover the pan and cook the peas very slowly until tender, which should not take more than 10 to 15 minutes. Sprinkle with minced parsley before serving. Serves two or three.

THE TEMPLE OF CONCORD — AGRIGENTO   *Sicily*

Almond Macaroons
Amaretti
(Almond paste, sugar, egg whites, pine nuts or candied fruit)

Cut ½ pound of commercial almond paste into small bits, and add 1 cup plus 2 tablespoons of fine granulated sugar and 2 unbeaten egg whites. Stir all together thoroughly until the mixture is smooth. Line a baking sheet with waxed paper and brush the paper with a little oil. Form the paste a spoonful at a time into rounds about 1 inch in diameter. Roll the top of each one in pine nuts, or dot them with finely diced candied fruits. Place the macaroons on the baking sheets, allowing space between them for spreading. Bake them in a 325° oven for 15 to 20 minutes. Remove them from the paper while they are still warm.

66

MAIORI, ON THE AMALFI DRIVE   *Campania*

Spaghetti with Fresh Tomato Sauce

Spaghetti alla Marinara

(Spaghetti, olive oil, onions, garlic, tomatoes, basil, anchovies)

Cook 1 pound of spaghetti (*see* Index), and serve it with the following sauce: Heat ¼ cup of olive oil in a heavy pot or skillet. Add 2 thinly sliced onions and cook them over low heat until soft and lightly browned. Add 3 minced cloves of garlic and cook another minute. Then add 6 large ripe tomatoes, peeled and cut in pieces (or 1 No. 3 can of Italian plum tomatoes), salt and pepper, and 4 leaves of fresh basil (or a good pinch of dried basil). Cook the sauce over high heat for about 10 minutes; the tomatoes should be soft but still fresh tasting and juicy. Then pour the sauce over the hot spaghetti, mix the two together at the table, and serve with grated Italian cheese if desired. Some Italian cooks also add 2 or 3 cut-up anchovy fillets to this sauce 5 minutes before it is finished. Serves four to six.

67

CESENATICO   *Emilia-Romagna*

Skewered Shrimp with Ham
Scampi con Prosciutto alla Griglia

(Shrimp, brandy, pepper, sage, prosciutto, olive oil, bread crumbs, lemon)

Peel and devein 20 raw jumbo shrimp. Sprinkle them with 3 to 4 tablespoons of brandy and let them stand for an hour. Then season them with a little freshly ground pepper and powdered sage, or put a leaf of fresh sage on each one. Roll each shrimp in a thin slice of *prosciutto* or ham, and thread them on 4 small skewers. Place them under a moderate pre-heated broiler until the ham begins to cook, turning them once; this will take about 3 to 5 minutes. Now dip each skewer in a little olive oil, roll it in fine bread crumbs, and broil them again until the crumbs are brown and the shrimp are cooked. Serve with wedges of lemon. Serves four.

DOCK AT CHIOGGIA

Veneto

Baked Tomatoes
Pomidori Ammollicati

(Tomatoes, bread crumbs, parsley, garlic, olive oil)

Cut 6 firm medium-size tomatoes in half crosswise, and place them cut side up in a shallow, well-oiled baking dish. Season them with salt and pepper. Combine ½ cup of dry bread crumbs, 1 tablespoon of finely chopped parsley, and 1 minced clove of garlic. Cover the tomatoes with this mixture, and sprinkle them generously with olive oil. Bake them in a 400° oven for about 10 minutes, or until they are lightly browned. Do not overcook them. Serves six.

69

WINE SHOP — ALASSIO   *Liguria*

Spaghetti with Oil and Garlic

Spaghetti al Olio ed Aglio

(Spaghetti, olive oil, garlic, parsley)

The cooking of spaghetti is extremely important though perfectly simple: Allow 3 to 4 ounces per person. For 1 pound of spaghetti bring at least 6 quarts of salted water to a rolling boil in a large kettle. Add the spaghetti, bring the water back to a boil, and cook the spaghetti until it is just tender and still somewhat firm, the stage called *al dente* by the Italians. This takes about 8 minutes for most varieties, but tasting is the only sure method. Never overcook it, and add 1 tablespoon of oil to the pot for the last 2 minutes of cooking to keep the spaghetti from sticking together when it is drained. Drain it and pour it into a heated serving dish.

Meanwhile, in a small saucepan, heat but do not boil ½ cup of the best quality of olive oil. Turn off the heat, add 2 to 4 finely minced cloves of garlic, according to taste, and let it stand for about a minute. Then add ½ cup of finely minced parsley, stir this sauce into the hot spaghetti, and serve at once. Serve with grated Parmesan if desired, though in Italy spaghetti prepared in this way is usually eaten without cheese. Serves four to six.

GALLIPOLI   *Apulia*

Potato and Onion Salad
Insalata di Patate e Cipolle

(Potatoes, onion, olive oil, wine vinegar, parsley, capers)

Boil 4 medium potatoes in their skins until done but still firm. Peel and slice them thinly while they are still warm, place them in a glass bowl, and season them with salt and freshly ground pepper. Slice very thinly 1 large mild red Italian onion, and add it to the potatoes. Mix together 4 tablespoons of olive oil and 1 tablespoon of wine vinegar, and pour this over the salad. Add 1 tablespoon of finely chopped parsley and toss the salad lightly. Then sprinkle a few capers over the top and let the salad stand 1 hour before serving. If you wish to make a more substantial dish of this, you may add a small can of tuna fish in oil, drained and flaked. Serves three or four.

TEMPLE OF CERES — PAESTUM   *Campania*

Cream of Tomato Soup
Zuppa di Pomodoro

(Onions, olive oil, tomatoes, parsley, basil, sour cream, Italian broth)

Sauté 2 chopped onions in 3 tablespoons of olive oil until they are soft and pale gold. Add 4 large peeled tomatoes, cut in pieces, a sprig of parsley, 2 or 3 fresh basil leaves, 2 teaspoons of sugar, and salt and pepper to taste. Cover, and simmer the vegetables for about 20 minutes, stirring occasionally; then force them through a fine sieve. When the purée is cool, stir in 1 cup of sour cream. Heat 1½ cups of chicken stock (or Italian broth; *see* Index), and add the tomato-cream mixture to it. Bring the soup barely to a boil (sour cream may curdle if it is boiled or overheated) and serve immediately. Serves four.

72

OSPEDALE DEL CEPPO — PISTOIA   *Tuscany*

Stuffed Tomatoes

Pomidori Ripieni

(Tomatoes, hard-boiled eggs, tuna fish, capers, parsley, mayonnaise)

Wash 4 large firm ripe tomatoes, cut a slice from the stem end of each, and shake out all the seeds and liquid. Combine: 2 hard-boiled eggs, chopped; 1 3½-ounce can of tuna fish, shredded; 1 teaspoon of salted Italian capers, rinsed and dried; 1 teaspoon of finely chopped parsley; and a dash of pepper and 2 to 3 tablespoons of good mayonnaise. Fill each tomato loosely with the mixture, mounding it on the tops. Add a dab of mayonnaise and a sprig of parsley. Serve chilled, on leaves of green lettuce. Serves four.

THE ARCADE—BOLOGNA   *Emilia-Romagna*

Tagliatelle with Ham

Tagliatelle al Prosciutto alla Bolognese

(Egg noodles, butter, prosciutto or ham, Parmesan)

Wherever you find a recipe for *tagliatelle* or *fettuccine,* which are practically identical, narrow egg noodles are meant. Use the packaged kind, or make Home-made *Pasta;* Italian housewives usually make their own.

In a large kettle of salted water boil 1 pound of egg noodles, taking care not to overcook them. Melt 7 tablespoons of butter in a saucepan. Sweet unsalted butter is best for this dish, and it should be heated only until it is just hot; do not let it boil or brown as this will completely change the taste you want to achieve. Add to the butter ¾ cup of ham or *prosciutto,* cut in very small dice. Drain the *tagliatelle,* add them to the melted butter, add ⅓ cup of grated Parmesan cheese, and toss all together. Serve at once. Serves six.

74

TRAJAN'S FORUM   *Rome*

Chicken Roman Style
Pollo alla Romana

(Chicken, olive oil, prosciutto, garlic, rosemary, red wine, tomatoes, stock)

Have a 3½- to 4-pound chicken cut in serving pieces. Wipe them dry and season them with salt and pepper. In a heavy pan heat 2 tablespoons of olive oil, and in it brown the pieces of chicken slowly on all sides, together with 2 slices of *prosciutto* (or ham or bacon), cut in small pieces. When the chicken is brown, add 1 small clove of garlic, chopped, ¼ teaspoon of rosemary, and ¾ cup of red wine. Simmer until the wine is almost evaporated, then add 4 medium tomatoes, peeled and cut in pieces, and ¼ cup of hot chicken stock or water. Cook the chicken for about 20 minutes more, or until it is tender, and remove it to a hot platter. Reduce the sauce over a brisk flame until it is slightly thickened, taste for seasoning, and pour it over the chicken. Serves four.

SANTA MARIA NOVELLA — FLORENCE   *Tuscany*

Italian Broth

Brodo

(Boiling fowl, veal shinbone, onion, carrot, leek, celery, parsley)

This light and delicate stock is the base for many soups and combinations which make it more than just a cup of broth. It is used, for instance, for *straciatella,* for *zuppa alla pavese,* and for *zuppa di pomodoro* (*see* Index).

In a soup kettle put a 5-pound boiling fowl, a piece of veal shinbone with some meat on it (or a knuckle of veal), and 2½ quarts of water; bring to a boil gradually and skim. Then add 1 onion and 1 carrot, both cut in large pieces, 1 leek, 1 stalk of celery with its leaves, a sprig of parsley, 1 teaspoon of salt, and a dash of pepper. Cover partially and keep at the lowest possible simmer for 2½ hours, skimming occasionally. Remove the fowl and reserve it for other purposes. Continue cooking the broth for another hour, or until it is flavorful and somewhat reduced. Strain and cool it, then chill in the refrigerator. Remove all fat from the surface before using.

76

ROMANESQUE DOORWAYS — TUSCANIA   *Latium*

Green Beans Sauté

Fagiolini Trifolati

(Green beans, parsley, garlic, butter, olive oil, nutmeg, Parmesan)

Wash 1 pound of fresh green beans, remove the stem ends, but leave the beans whole. Cook them slowly, covered, in a little salted water until the water has evaporated and the beans are cooked but still firm. In a mortar mash well together 1 tablespoon of minced parsley and 1 minced clove of garlic. In a heavy shallow saucepan (a "sauté" pan) heat together 2 tablespoons of butter and 1 tablespoon of olive oil. Add the parsley and garlic mixture, stir well, and cook for about 10 seconds. Then add the beans, salt, pepper, and a pinch of nutmeg. Toss the beans to coat them well, cover, and cook over low heat for about 5 minutes. Just before serving, stir in 1 tablespoon of grated Parmesan. Turn the beans out into a hot serving dish, sprinkle them with minced parsley, and serve at once. Serves four.

THE DOLOMITES NEAR CAMPITELLO   *Trentino-Alto Adige*

Cucumber and Green Pepper Salad
Antipasto di Cetrioli e Peperoni

(Cucumbers, green pepper, mushrooms, eggs, oil, vinegar, mayonnaise)

Peel 2 cucumbers, slice them very thinly, sprinkle them with salt, and let them stand for an hour under pressure. Clean and slice very thinly one large green pepper, and season it with a dressing made of 1 part wine vinegar, 3 parts olive oil, and salt and pepper. Slice 4 large mushrooms and dress them in the same way. Drain the cucumbers, place them in a layer in a deep dish, and season them with oil and vinegar only. Over them spread the green pepper, and on this put the mushrooms. Over all spread a layer of the best homemade mayonnaise, made with olive oil and lemon juice. Cut 2 hard-boiled eggs lengthwise into wedges and place these around the edge of the dish. This makes a first course, or *antipasto*, for four.

78

TEMPLE OF NEPTUNE—PAESTUM   *Campania*

Spring Vegetable Salad

Antipasto di Primavera

(Lima beans, peas, artichokes, potatoes, mayonnaise, eggs, capers, pickles)

Shell 2 pounds each of tender young lima beans and peas; cook them in the usual way in salted boiling water. Slice thinly half a package of frozen baby artichokes, and cook them briefly in water with a little vinegar. Boil or steam a little less than ½ pound of small new potatoes; cool, peel, and slice them. When all the vegetables are cooled, mix them together gently in a bowl with a dressing made of one part wine vinegar, three parts olive oil, and salt and pepper to taste. Let them stand for an hour or two. Make a mayonnaise seasoned with a little mixed mustard and chopped fresh tarragon; lacking this, use tarragon vinegar. Put the salad in a serving dish, spread the mayonnaise over it, and decorate with slices of hard-boiled egg, capers, and a few slices of sour gherkin. Serve as a first course or as a salad. Serves six.

79

MONTELEONE D'ORVIETO   *Umbria*

Veal Cutlets with Marsala

Scaloppine al Marsala

(Veal cutlets, flour, butter, Marsala)

Pound 8 small thin veal cutlets between two sheets of waxed paper to flatten them as much as possible. Season them with salt and pepper, dip them lightly in flour, and sauté them over a brisk fire in 4 tablespoons of hot butter. When they are golden brown on each side, remove them to a hot platter. Stir 4 tablespoons of Marsala into the remaining juices, bring the sauce just to a boil, and pour it over the cutlets. Serves three or four.

FARM NEAR FERRARA   *Emilia-Romagna*

Egg-and-Butter Cream Charlotte
Budino di Uova in Ghiaccio
(Hard-boiled egg yolks, butter, sugar, vanilla, rum, lady fingers, cream)

Cream together well 4 tablespoons of soft butter and ¼ cup of fine granulated sugar. Add the yolks of 6 hard-boiled eggs, a few drops of vanilla extract, and 1 tablespoon of rum, and cream all together until smooth. Butter a small mold, and line it with split lady fingers first dipped in a little rum. Fill the center with the egg-and-butter cream, and chill well. Serve the charlotte unmolded on a platter, and pass whipped cream separately. Serves four.

RAVELLO   *Campania*

Braised Sweetbreads with Peas
Animelle in Humido con Piselli

(Sweetbreads, butter, white wine, flour, chicken stock, parsley, peas)

Put 2 pairs of sweetbreads in a saucepan with cold water to cover and salt and a little lemon juice. Bring the water slowly to a boil, then simmer the sweetbreads for 10 minutes. Drain them, remove skin and filaments, and wipe them dry. Heat 2 tablespoons of butter in a sauté pan, and in it brown the sweetbreads lightly on all sides. Add ⅓ cup of dry white wine and simmer slowly until the wine is almost evaporated. Then stir in 2 teaspoons of flour and add gradually ¾ cup of hot chicken stock (or Italian Broth). Cover the saucepan and cook the sweetbreads slowly for about 30 minutes. Shortly before they are done, add 2 teaspoons of finely minced parsley and taste for seasoning.

Meanwhile, shell 2 pounds of peas and put them in a saucepan with 2 tablespoons of melted butter. Stir them briefly, on the fire, then add about ½ cup of chicken stock (or Italian Broth), cover the pan, and cook the peas slowly until they are tender, adding more liquid if necessary. Season them with salt to taste. Serve the sweetbreads on a hot platter, with their sauce and surrounded by the peas. Serves four.

BASILICA OF SAN FRANCESCO—ASSISI   *Umbria*

Italian Rice with Mushrooms

Risotto coi Funghi

(Rice, oil, butter, onion, garlic, stock, mushrooms, parsley, Parmesan)

Make a standard *risotto* or Italian rice: In a heavy casserole heat together 2 tablespoons each of olive oil and butter. Add 1 small chopped onion and cook it slowly until it is pale gold. Add 1 minced clove of garlic and 1 cup of raw rice, and stir to coat all the grains. Then add 1 cup of boiling stock, and simmer very slowly, covered, until the stock is absorbed. Now add 2½ more cups of stock, cover, and cook very slowly until done. Stir once or twice with a large fork.

Meanwhile, rinse, dry, and slice thinly ¾ pound of mushrooms. Sauté them slowly in 3½ tablespoons of hot butter for about 5 minutes. Add 2 teaspoons of finely minced parsley and salt and pepper, and cook for 2 or 3 more minutes, until the liquid has evaporated. When the *risotto* is three-quarters cooked, stir in the mushrooms and finish the cooking. Then add a lump of butter and ¼ cup of grated Parmesan cheese. Cover the rice until it is served, and sprinkle more Parmesan on top just before serving. Serves four.

SCILLA   *Calabria*

Anchovy Sauce

Salsa con Acciughe

(Anchovies, olive oil, garlic, hard-boiled-egg yolks, parsley, pepper, vinegar)

In a small saucepan warm 2 tablespoons of olive oil, add 8 anchovy fillets, chopped, and 1 small clove of garlic, chopped and mashed. Let these steep together over the lowest possible heat until the anchovies dissolve. Mash the yolks of 4 hard-boiled eggs with ¼ cup of finely minced parsley, and add a dash of freshly ground black pepper. Stir in gradually 2 tablespoons of wine vinegar and the anchovy, garlic, and oil mixture, blending all together well. The sauce should be the consistency of a thin mayonnaise; if it is too thick, thin it with a few drops of hot water and a few drops of vinegar. Cool it, and serve it with cold poached fish or cold veal or pork. Serves four.

84

AMALFI   *Campania*

Steamed-Clam Soup

Zuppa di Vongole

(Clams, tomato juice, olive oil, herbs, cayenne)

The Italians call all sorts of things *zuppa*; this "soup" is quite substantial enough for a main dish: Scrub 2 dozen clams and put them in a deep saucepan. Add ½ cup each of water and tomato juice, ¼ cup of olive oil, ½ teaspoon of minced parsley, and ¼ teaspoon of orégano. Cover the saucepan and cook the clams over high heat until the shells open. Remove them to two large soup plates. Add a pinch of cayenne pepper to the broth, pour it over the clams, and serve at once, with toasted Italian bread. Serves two.

LANDSCAPE NEAR AIELLO   *Calabria*

Crepe Batter

Crepes

(Eggs, oil, cream, flour, salt, water)

Beat together 2 eggs, ¾ tablespoon of oil, and 1½ tablespoons of heavy cream. Combine this gradually with 6 tablespoons of sifted flour and ¼ teaspoon of salt. Mix this well until it is perfectly smooth, then add very gradually ¼ cup of cold water. The batter should have the consistency of thin cream. Let it rest for 2 hours in the refrigerator before using it; if it thickens up, you may add gradually, stirring well, a few more drops of water to bring it to the right consistency. Melt a little butter in a 6-inch frying pan, and make the crepes one by one, pouring in about 2 tablespoons of batter for each one and turning it once to brown on both sides. Melt a little butter again in the pan before starting each crepe. This amount of batter should make eight. See Crepes in the Index for typically Italian ways to stuff them.

THE FORTIFIED HARBOR—GALLIPOLI   *Apulia*

Spaghetti with Clam Sauce

Spaghetti con le Vongole

(Oil, garlic, herbs, tomatoes, clams, spaghetti)

Heat ¼ cup of olive oil in a saucepan, and add 2 chopped and mashed cloves of garlic. Cook them over a slow fire until they are pale gold, then add 2 tablespoons of minced parsley, 1 teaspoon of fresh marjoram (or ⅓ teaspoon of dried marjoram), and a few leaves of basil. Stir briefly and add 2 pounds of peeled, seeded, and coarsely chopped tomatoes (or 2 generous cups of canned Italian tomatoes). Meanwhile, steam open 3 pints of fresh hard-shell clams, and remove them from their shells. Let the clam juice rest in the pot to settle the sand, then pour off the juice and strain it through a cloth. Add it to the tomato mixture and simmer the sauce for about 45 minutes, or until it has thickened to a good consistency. Chop the clams, add them to the tomato sauce, and cook them in it very briefly; they need almost no cooking, since they have already been steamed. Season the sauce with a good dash of pepper and a little salt if needed. This makes enough sauce for 1 pound of spaghetti, to serve six. Pour the sauce over the freshly cooked spaghetti, and serve immediately. The Italians do not serve grated cheese with this sauce.

If you cannot get fresh clams, use canned minced clams which give very good results. Drain the juice from two 7½-ounce cans and add it to the sauce with the tomatoes. Add the minced clams at the end, just as you would the fresh ones.

HILL TOWN OF ITRI   *Campania*

Purée of Potatoes
Purea di Patate
(Potatoes, butter, onion, milk, nutmeg, Parmesan)

Scrub 2 pounds of potatoes and boil them, unpeeled, in salted water to cover for about 25 minutes, or until tender. Drain and peel them, force them through a sieve, and beat them until smooth. In a saucepan brown a slice of onion in 2½ tablespoons of butter, remove the onion, discard it, and add the mashed potatoes to the remaining butter. Cook them briefly, then stir them well and gradually stir in about ½ cup of hot milk. When the purée comes away from the sides of the pan, remove it from the fire and beat in salt, pepper, a dash of nutmeg, and 2 tablespoons of grated Parmesan cheese. Return to the fire briefly and stir to blend in the cheese. Serves six.

HARBOR AT MOLFETTA   *Apulia*

Veal Stew

Stufatino di Vitello

(Veal, olive oil, garlic, tomatoes, rosemary, basil, white wine)

Have 2 pounds of leg of veal cut into 2-inch cubes. Heat ¼ cup of olive oil in a heavy saucepan, and add the veal and 1 chopped clove of garlic. Turn the meat from time to time to sear it on all sides. Add about 1½ cups of Italian plum tomatoes, drained, a little salt and pepper, a sprig of rosemary, 2 leaves of fresh basil, and ½ cup of dry white wine. Cover the saucepan and simmer the stew over a very low fire for about 1¾ hours, or until the veal is tender. If the sauce reduces too much, add a little hot water; or, at the last, if the sauce is too liquid, transfer the meat to a hot serving dish and reduce the sauce over a brisk fire. In either case, remove the meat before serving and strain the sauce. Serves four.

MASSALUBRENSE   *Campania*

Steamed Mussels with Tomatoes

Datteri di Mare a Stufato

(Mussels or clams, olive oil, parsley, garlic, tomatoes)

Clean 2 quarts of mussels very thoroughly, scrubbing them well and removing the "beards." Spread them in a shallow layer in a broad pan, cover the pan, and put it over moderate heat, shaking it occasionally, just until the mussels open. Strain the juice through a double layer of cheese cloth and reserve it. Remove the mussels from their shells, rinse them with a dash of hot salted water to clean off any remaining grains of sand, and drain them well. Heat ⅓ cup of olive oil in an earthern casserole. Add 2 generous tablespoons of minced parsley and 1 minced clove of garlic. Cook these together slowly for 2 or 3 minutes, then add 2 medium tomatoes, peeled, seeded, and coarsely chopped, salt and pepper, and a little of the reserved mussel liquor. Cover, and cook the mixture slowly for another 10 minutes. Now add the mussels and cook them, covered, for 5 or 6 minutes. Serve in the casserole. Serves four. You can also prepare clams in this way.

90

ALBEROBELLO   *Apulia*

"Cooked Water" Soup

Aqua Cotta

(Mushrooms, garlic, oil, tomatoes, water, eggs, Parmesan, croutons)

Recipes for *aqua cotta* are numerous and varied but are always made up of combinations of vegetables sautéed in oil and then cooked with water rather than stock. The eggs and croutons are also invariable. The combination presented below we find to be one of the best, though we have also enjoyed another very good one composed of onions, celery, tomatoes, and sweet peppers.

Clean and slice 1 pound of mushrooms, discarding the stems, and sauté them slowly with a clove of garlic in ½ cup of olive oil for 5 to 6 minutes. Remove the garlic, salt the mushrooms, and add 4 medium-large tomatoes, peeled, seeded, and coarsely chopped. Continue cooking the mixture for 15 minutes. Then add 4 cups of water, cover the soup, and simmer it for 1 hour. Taste for seasoning, and boil the soup down a little, uncovered, if it is too thin. In the bottom of a soup tureen, beat together 3 eggs and 3 tablespoons of grated Parmesan. Stir in the "cooked water" soup, and serve it at once with crisp slices of French or Italian bread fried in butter or oil. Serves four.

WASHDAY AT VINTIMIGLIA   *Liguria*

Rice with Shrimp
Risotto di Scampi
(Shrimp, wine, onion, celery, carrot, herbs, butter, oil, rice, garlic, Parmesan)

Shell ¾ pound of raw shrimp. Simmer the shells in 1 quart of water and 1 cup of white wine combined, together with a fish head or other fish scraps if you have them, and 1 small onion, 1 stalk of celery, a few slices of carrot, a sprig of parsley, 1 bay leaf, and salt and pepper. Simmer this stock for ½ hour, then strain it. Heat together 2 tablespoons each of butter and olive oil, and stir in 1 cup of raw rice. When it is golden, add 1 cup of the hot fish stock, cover, and simmer until the liquid is absorbed. Then add another 2½ cups of stock. Cook 1 minced clove of garlic and 1 teaspoon of minced parsley for 2 minutes in 1 tablespoon of olive oil, and add this to the *risotto*. Cover the saucepan and cook slowly for 10 minutes. Then add the shrimp, cover again, and cook until all the liquid is absorbed. Add a good lump of butter, ¼ cup of grated Parmesan cheese, stir together with a fork, and serve at once. Serves four.

92

SPOLETO   *Umbria*

Truffle Sauce for Spaghetti

Spaghetti alla Spoletina

(Spaghetti, truffles, anchovies, parsley, olive oil, garlic, tomato paste)

For ¾ pound of spaghetti to serve four: Chop 3 or 4 ounces of truffles (two 50-gram cans of black truffles or white Italian truffles) and mash them to a paste in a mortar with 3 anchovy fillets and 1 teaspoon of chopped parsley. Heat ⅜ cup of olive oil with 1 cut clove of garlic and let this stand for 5 or 6 minutes. Remove the garlic and add the truffle mixture to the oil. Dilute 4 tablespoons of tomato paste in 1 cup of warm water and stir this into the first mixture. Add salt to taste, and heat the sauce slowly just to the boiling point. Pour over the hot spaghetti and serve at once.

HILL TOWN OF OSIMO   *Marche*

Stuffed Eggs

Uova Ripiene

(Eggs, butter, mustard, capers, anchovies)

Slice hard-boiled eggs in half lengthwise and remove the yolks. In a bowl blend the yolks with a little softened butter, French mustard, salt and pepper, and a few chopped capers. Use the salted Italian capers, first rinsed and dried. If the mixture is too dry, add a few drops of good Italian olive oil. Fill the whites with this mixture. Decorate each one with an anchovy fillet first cut in half lengthwise, then laid crisscross on the egg; place a caper at each end. Serve with assorted *antipasti*.

94

SEACOAST VILLAGE   *Calabria*

Chicken Livers with Prosciutto and Sage
Fegatini di Pollo alla Salvia

(Chicken livers, butter, prosciutto, sage, Marsala, croutons)

Allow 1 pound of chicken livers to serve four. Cut each one into three pieces. Cut 4 slices of bread into triangles and fry these on both sides in butter. Heat 4 tablespoons of butter in a skillet, and put in the chicken livers. Add salt and pepper, 2 slices of *prosciutto* or ham, cut in fine slivers, and 1 teaspoon of chopped fresh sage leaves or ½ teaspoon of dried sage. Stir lightly, and cook the chicken livers for about 5 minutes; be sure not to overcook them. Arrange the bread croutons on a hot platter, and transfer the chicken livers from the pan to the croutons with a slotted spoon. Add 1 tablespoon of Marsala to the pan juices, reheat them, stirring well, and spoon this sauce over the chicken livers. Serves four.

FLOWER STAND — GENOA   *Liguria*

Chicken Sauté Aretina
Pollo all'Aretina

(Chicken, butter, olive oil, onion, bacon, white wine, stock, rice, fresh peas)

    Cut a frying chicken into serving pieces. In a heavy pan, brown them slowly on all sides in 2 tablespoons of butter first heated with 2 tablespoons of olive oil. Add salt and pepper, 1 finely chopped onion, and ½ tablespoon of diced bacon. Brown these a little, being careful not to burn the onion. Add ¾ cup of white wine, bring it to a boil, and let it simmer for 3 to 5 minutes. Add 1 cup of hot chicken stock, and when the liquid boils again, add ½ cup of rice and ¾ cup of shelled fresh peas. Cover the pan closely, and cook the mixture over a very low fire for 25 minutes or more. Add a little boiling water if the liquid dries up before the vegetables and chicken are tender. Taste for seasoning. Serves four.

THE TIBER   *Rome*

Spinach Borghese

Spinaci alla Borghese

(Spinach, butter, anchovies, garlic, pepper, nutmeg)

Wash and stem 1 pound of fresh spinach. Cook it down slowly with no more water than remains on the leaves. When it is soft, drain it thoroughly, chop it fine and press out any remaining water. In a saucepan heat 2 tablespoons of butter, and add 4 chopped anchovy fillets and 1 cut clove of garlic. Cook together slowly until the anchovies have almost dissolved. Remove the garlic, add the spinach to the pan, and season with freshly ground pepper and a dash of nutmeg, but no salt. Add 1 tablespoon of butter, and stir all together until the spinach is reheated. Serves four.

THE TOWN HALL—ORTA   *Piedmont*

Shrimp Salad Antipasto

Antipasto di Scampi

(Shrimp, mayonnaise, sour cream, ketchup, brandy, chicory)

Boil ¾ pound of shrimp in salted water for 5 minutes. Drain, shell, and devein them. Mix together ½ cup of mayonnaise, ½ cup of sour cream, 2 tablespoons of tomato ketchup or chili sauce, and 2 teaspoons of brandy. Combine the shrimp and sauce. In four small deep dishes or bowls place a layer of hearts of chicory, first well washed, drained, and chopped into small pieces. Place the shrimps and their sauce on the beds of chicory, and chill for half an hour before serving. Serves four.

VILLAGE CHURCH—PRAIANO   *Campania*

Biscuit Tortoni

Tortoni

(Egg white, cream, sugar, macaroons, rum, almonds)

Beat 1 egg white stiff, adding gradually 3 tablespoons of confectioners' sugar. Beat 1 cup of heavy cream until thick but not stiff together with 3 tablespoons of confectioners' sugar. Mix ½ cup of macaroon crumbs into the cream. (To make these, dry macaroons slowly in the oven, then crush them finely with a rolling pin.) Add 2 teaspoons of rum to the macaroon cream, beat it again a little, and fold in the egg white. Pack the mixture into heavy fluted paper cups, and sprinkle the tops with unsalted chopped toasted almonds. Put the *tortoni* in a freezer tray, and keep in the freezing compartment of the refrigerator until firm. Serves four.

BASSANO DI GRAPPA   *Veneto*

Shirred Eggs with Chicken Livers
Uova al Piatto all'Emiliana
(Eggs, butter, chicken livers, Marsala)

Butter 4 shirred-egg dishes and break an egg into each one. Season the eggs with a little salt and pepper, and put them in a 350° oven for 10 to 12 minutes, or until the whites are set but the yolks are still soft. Meanwhile, cut 6 chicken livers into quarters, or smaller if you wish, and cook these in 4 tablespoons of hot butter for 1 to 2 minutes, turning them to cook on all sides. Season them with salt and pepper and add ¼ cup of Marsala. Simmer the mixture for about 30 seconds. (Chicken livers should not be overcooked or they will be tough.) Spoon the chicken livers and their juices over each egg and serve at once. Serves four.

VIA GUICCIARDINI — FLORENCE   *Tuscany*

Tomato Sauce
Salsa di Pomodoro
(Olive oil, onions, carrot, garlic, herbs, tomatoes, meat stock)

Heat ¼ cup of olive oil and in it cook 2 medium onions, sliced, until they are soft and transparent. Add 1 small grated carrot, 1 minced clove of garlic, and 1 teaspoon of minced parsley. Cook together slowly for 3 minutes, then add 2 pounds of fresh tomatoes, coarsely chopped, salt and pepper, a dash of celery salt, several leaves of fresh basil, ⅓ teaspoon dried thyme, and ½ cup of meat stock. Simmer the sauce, covered, for about 1¼ hours; stir it from time to time. When it is fairly thick, force it through a fine strainer. This sauce may be used with any dish calling for tomato sauce, or with 1 pound of cooked spaghetti. Serves four to six.

101

ANTIQUITIES OF THE ROMAN FORUM   *Rome*

Salmis of Duck Roman Style

Anitra in Salmi alla Romana

(Duck, onion, cloves, sage, bay leaf, oil, vinegar, croutons)

Cut a duck into serving pieces and wash and dry them. Cook the pieces slowly in
an iron skillet for 10 or more minutes to render the fat. Turn them from time to
time and prick the skin to release the fat. Remove the duck and discard the fat. In
a heavy casserole put 1 whole onion stuck with 3 cloves, a good pinch of sage, 1
crumbled bay leaf, and the chopped liver, heart, and gizzard of the duck. Add the
pieces of duck, salt and pepper, and ⅓ cup each of olive oil and wine vinegar. Seal
the casserole as hermetically as possible with a piece of heavy aluminum foil, put
on the lid, and cook the duck over low heat (or in a 275° oven) for about 1 hour,
until it is tender; add a little hot water to the casserole if necessary before the duck
is done. Arrange the duck on a hot platter, surrounded by triangles of bread fried
in butter. Remove some of the fat from the sauce, strain the sauce, and pour it over
the duck. Serves four.

CETARA, ON THE AMALFI DRIVE   *Campania*

Fish with Rice in Shells
Conchigli di Pesce al Riso

(Fish, shellfish, rice, butter, Parmesan, cream sauce, egg)

A delicious little dish to use up left-over fish with rice; it is baked in scallop shells. Heat 1 cup of cooked rice with a little butter and grated Parmesan cheese. Flake enough cooked fish to make 1 cup; any delicate white fish will be good, especially if you can mix with it a little cooked shellfish (shrimp, or sliced scallops, or diced lobster or crab meat). Butter 4 scallop shells or small ramekins, and put a layer of rice and then one of fish in each one. Make ½ cup of cream sauce by blending 1 scant tablespoon of flour into 1 tablespoon of melted butter, and adding salt and pepper and, gradually, ½ cup of warm milk. When the sauce thickens, off the fire stir in 1 beaten egg. Spoon this sauce over the filled shells, sprinkle with grated Parmesan, and dot with butter. Bake the shells in a 400° oven for about 10 minutes. Serves four.

103

PORTOFINO   *Liguria*

Sea Bass in Wine Sauce
Branzino al Vino Bianco

(Sea bass, flour, olive oil, shallots, anchovies, parsley, white wine, stock)

Cut 2 pounds of fillets of sea bass into serving pieces, season them with salt and pepper, and roll them lightly in flour. Heat 4 tablespoons of olive oil in a skillet and cook the fish in this, over moderate heat, until the pieces are brown on both sides and cooked through. Meanwhile, in another saucepan, heat 2 tablespoons of olive oil, add 2 chopped shallots, 2 chopped anchovy fillets, and 1 teaspoon of minced parsley. Simmer slowly until softened, add 1 cup of dry white wine, and simmer the mixture again until the wine is reduced by one quarter. Then add ¼ cup of chicken stock and salt (sparingly) and pepper to taste, and simmer the sauce for another 3 or 4 minutes. Pour it over the fish and simmer all together for a minute or two to blend the flavors. Serves four.

STONE QUARRY NEAR MATERA   *Basilicata*

Sweet-and-Sour Eggplant and Tomato Hors-d'Oeuvre
Caponata

(Eggplant, celery, onion, olive oil, tomato sauce, spices, sugar, vinegar)

Peel 2 meduim cggplants, cut them into 1-inch dice, sprinkle these with salt and let them stand for an hour. Dice 4 stalks of celery very small, parboil in boiling water for 2 minutes, drain, and measure out 1 cup of the celery. Slice 3 medium onions thinly. Rinse and dry the diced eggplant and sauté it in 1 cup of hot olive oil about 10 minutes, until it is lightly browned; remove the eggplant with a slotted spoon and reserve it. Add another ½ cup of olive oil to the pan, heat it, and sauté the sliced onions in it until they are soft but not browned. Then add the cup of parboiled celery and ¾ cup of tomato sauce or tomato purée, and simmer the mixture for 15 minutes, stirring often.

Now add: 2 tablespoons of salted Italian capers, rinsed and drained; a dozen black Italian olives, pitted and finely chopped; and 1 tablespoon of pine nuts. Heat ¼ cup of red-wine vinegar, dissolve in it 2 tablespoons of sugar and ½ teaspoon of salt, and add a good dash of freshly ground pepper. Add this last mixture to the *caponata,* add the sautéed eggplant, and simmer it, covered, over low heat and stirring often, for 20 minutes, until it is thick and condensed; have a little extra tomato sauce handy to add in case it should get *too* dry. *Caponata* should be dark and pungently sweet and sour. Serve it chilled, as an hors-d'oeuvre, with crusty Italian bread.

GIFT SHOP—TAORMINA   *Sicily*

Green Italian Rice

Risotto Verde

(Italian Rice, butter, onion, carrot, celery, spinach, mushrooms, nutmeg, Parmesan)

Heat 2 tablespoons of butter in a frying pan, add 1 small chopped onion, and cook it slowly until it is pale gold. Add ½ a small carrot, finely grated, ½ a small stalk of celery, thinly sliced, 3 tablespoons of chopped raw spinach, and 3 or 4 sliced mushrooms. Cook the vegetables over low heat for 5 or 6 minutes.

Start a *risotto* (Italian Rice; *see* Index) with 1 cup of rice; when the rice has been stirred into the oil and butter and taken on a pale golden color, add the vegetable mixture, and a dash of nutmeg, pepper, and a little salt. Then add the hot broth and continue cooking the *risotto* in the usual way. When it is done, add 1 tablespoon of finely minced parsley, a good lump of butter, and ¼ cup of grated Parmesan cheese, stirring carefully with a fork. Cover the rice until it is served. Serves four.

106

MAIN STREET OF ALASSIO   *Liguria*

Crepes with Ricotta and Ham
Crepes con Ricotta e Prosciutto

(Crepe Batter, Ricotta, prosciutto or ham, milk, butter, Parmesan)

Make a Crepe Batter (*see* Index), let it rest for 2 hours, and make 8 crepes in the usual way. Mix ¾ cup of Ricotta cheese (or sieved cottage cheese) with 4 tablespoons of chopped *prosciutto* or ham. Add a little salt, and blend the mixture thoroughly, adding, a few drops at a time, just enough milk to make a soft paste. Put 2 tablespoons of the mixture in the center of each crepe, and roll them up. Place them side by side in a shallow buttered baking dish. Dot them generously with butter and sprinkle them with grated Parmesan. Bake the crepe in a 400° oven for about 10 minutes, or until they are lightly browned. Serves four.

ROMAN ROAD   *Rome*

Turkey Breast Cardinal
Filetti di Tacchino alla Cardinale

(Turkey breast, flour, butter, Marsala, stock, prosciutto, truffles, Parmesan)

Remove the meat of one side of raw turkey breast from the bone, and take off the skin. With a very sharp knife slice the meat into 4 to 6 fillets, and pound these between sheets of waxed paper to make them thin and even. Dust them with flour, salt, and pepper. In a large skillet, cook them slowly in 4 tablespoons of hot butter for about 5 minutes on each side. There should be plenty of butter, and do not let it darken or burn. Stir into the pan 1 tablespoon of Marsala and 4 to 6 tablespoons of chicken stock, spooning the liquid over the fillets. Place a thin slice of *prosciutto* or ham on each fillet and on this a layer of white Italian truffles, sliced paper thin. (Or use sliced mushrooms first sautéed for 2 minutes in butter in another pan.) Sprinkle a layer of grated Parmesan cheese over the fillets, and spoon a little of the liquid over each of them again. Cover the pan closely and heat until the cheese spreads a little. Serve the *filetti* at once with the pan juices spooned over them. Serves four to six.

If your supplier sells turkey in parts, buy the breast only for this dish. Or the *filetti* may be made with slices of cold roast turkey; in this case, only heat them in the hot butter, instead of cooking them for the full 5 minutes on each side.

108

LANDSCAPE NEAR GUBBIO   *Umbria*

Veal Cutlets Bolognese
Costolette Bolognese
(Veal cutlets, flour, salt, pepper, butter, Marsala, stock, Parmesan)

Pound 4 thin slices of veal even thinner between pieces of waxed paper. Dust them lightly with flour and season them with salt and pepper. Melt 2 tablespoons of butter in a frying pan and brown the cutlets in it: Cook them over a brisk fire for about 1 minute on each side, and do not allow the butter to burn. Then stir 1 tablespoon of hot water, 2 tablespoons of Marsala, and 2 tablespoons of stock into the pan. Lower the heat, spread a little grated Parmesan cheese over each piece of veal, and spoon the sauce over them. Cover the pan and continue cooking for 4 or 5 minutes. Serve the *costolette* at once, with the reduced pan juices poured over them. Serves two.

SORI, A MEDITERRANEAN VILLAGE   *Liguria*

Spinach with Oil, Genoa Style
Spinaci all'Olio Genovese

(Spinach, nutmeg, raisins, pine nuts, olive oil, parsley, anchovies, croutons)

Wash 2 pounds of spinach thoroughly. Cook it with just the water remaining on the leaves until it is soft. Drain it well, and chop it. Add salt and pepper and a dash of nutmeg. Meanwhile, soak ⅓ of a cup of seedless raisins in a little warm water to soften them. Drain them well and add them to the spinach. Add ¼ cup of pine nuts and mix all together well. In a saucepan heat ¼ cup of olive oil, add 2 tablespoons of finely chopped parsley and 4 anchovy fillets, cut in small pieces. Stir the mixture over a low fire until the anchovies are dissolved. Add the spinach, stir, cover the pan, and leave it over very low heat for 5 to 10 minutes to blend the flavors. Serve on triangles of bread fried in butter. Serves four.

DOCK AT CHIOGGIA   *Veneto Euganea*

Stuffed Striped Bass

Spinola Ripiena

(Bass, oil, onion, garlic, celery, bread crumbs, herbs, Parmesan, butter, lemon)

Heat ¼ cup of olive oil in a small saucepan, and in it sauté 1 onion and 1 clove of garlic, both finely chopped, and ½ cup of chopped celery. In about 10 minutes, or when the vegetables are soft and golden, combine them with 1¾ cups of coarse dry bread crumbs. Add salt, pepper, a pinch each of thyme and orègano, and ¼ cup of grated Parmesan cheese, and mix well together. Have a 3- to 4-pound striped bass cleaned, split, and the backbone removed. Salt the fish lightly, stuff it with the bread-crumb mixture, and sew up the opening. Place the fish in an oiled baking dish, brush it with oil, and dot it with butter. Bake it for 10 minutes in a 400° oven, then lower the heat to 325°, add ¼ cup of hot water to the pan, and cook the fish for another 20 to 30 minutes, or until the flesh can be flaked with a fork. Baste the bass occasionally as it bakes, and add the juice of a lemon to the pan a few minutes before it is done. Serves six.

111

HARBOR AT CAMOGLI   *Liguria*

Baked Fish with Green Herbs

Pesce Gratinato al Verde

(Fish fillets, parsley, chives, bread crumbs, olive oil, lemon)

In a shallow buttered baking dish arrange 2 pounds of fish fillets such as flounder, whiting, or other good, medium-size white fish. Season them with salt and
pepper, and sprinkle over them 3 tablespoons of minced parsley and 2 teaspoons
of finely cut chives. Add a thin layer of fine bread crumbs and sprinkle over all
⅜ cup or more of olive oil. Bake the fish in a 375° oven for 25 to 30 minutes.
Serve with wedges of lemon. Serves four.

BRONZOLO   *Trentino-Alto Adige*

Roast Chicken Bolognese

Pollo Arrosto alla Bolognese

(Chicken, butter, olive oil, prosciutto, garlic, rosemary, tomato, stock)

Truss a 4-pound chicken. In an iron casserole, heat 1 tablespoon each of butter and olive oil, and in this brown the chicken lightly on all sides. Add a finely diced slice of *prosciutto* or ham (containing both lean and fat), 1 cut clove or garlic, a sprig of rosemary, and salt and pepper. When the ham has browned a little, add 1 large peeled, seeded, and coarsely chopped tomato. Cook the chicken, uncovered, in a 300° oven, basting often, for about 1½ hours, or until tender when pierced with a fork. Add a small amount of stock to the pot from time to time if the juices reduce too much. Serve the chicken with diced potatoes browned in butter or bacon fat. Serves four.

MOUNTAIN HIGHWAY *Tuscany*

Fried Chicken Tuscany

Pollo Fritto alla Toscana

(Chicken, flour, egg, frying oil, parsley, lemon)

Cut a 3-pound broiler into eight pieces, wipe them dry, and season them with salt and pepper. Coat them lightly with flour and dip them in 2 eggs first beaten together with 2 teaspoons of olive oil. Fry the pieces in deep hot frying oil until they are brown and crisp. Serve them on a hot platter, sprinkled with chopped parsley and surrounded with wedges of lemon. Serves four.

114

THE BRIDGE OF SIGHS—VENICE *Veneto Euganea*

Peaches in White Wine

Pesche al Vino

(Peaches, white wine, sugar, Maraschino or rum)

Peel 6 large firm, ripe peaches, cut them in halves and remove the pits. Place them in a wide sauté pan. Combine ¾ cup of rather sweet white wine, such as a Sauternes, 6 tablespoons of sugar, and ⅓ cup of water. Pour this over the peaches and cook them over a low fire, covered, for 6 to 8 minutes, or until they are tender but not too soft. With a slotted spoon remove the peaches to a bowl, pour the syrup over them, and let them cool. Chill them well in the refrigerator. Pour 3 tablespoons of Maraschino or rum over the peaches before serving. Serves six.

THE CATHEDRAL—ORVIETO   *Umbria*

Italian Rice

Risotto

(Rice, butter, olive oil, onion, garlic, stock, Parmesan)

This recipe if for plain *risotto* and is delicious just as it is. It serves also as the basis for any more elaborate variation (including inventions of your own), no matter what other ingredients are added (*see* Index):

Over a moderate fire, in a heavy saucepan, heat together 2 tablespoons each of butter and olive oil. Add 1 small onion, chopped. When it is pale gold and transparent, add ½ or 1 small chopped and mashed clove of garlic, and stir in 1 cup of raw rice. Stir until the rice is light yellow and well coated with fat, then add 1 cup of boiling stock or Italian broth (*see* Index). Cover the pan tightly and simmer the *risotto* over a low fire until all the liquid is absorbed. Then gradually add another 2½ cups of hot stock (making 3½ cups in all, to 1 cup of rice.) Cover and simmer again slowly, stirring occasionally, until all the liquid is absorbed. Add a good lump of butter and ¼ cup of grated Parmesan cheese, stir lightly with a fork, sprinkle the top with another ¼ cup of Parmesan, and serve at once. Serves four.

PIAZZA DEL CAMPO — SIENA   *Tuscany*

Homemade Green Lasagne
Lasagne Verdi
(Flour, salt, eggs, spinach, water)

These are made in the same way as plain *lasagne* (*see* homemade *pasta* in the Index), but the ingredients are as follows: 4 cups of flour, 2 teaspoons of salt, 2 large eggs, ½ pound of fresh spinach, and only a few drops of water if needed to make the dough manageable. First, cook the spinach only until it is wilted, with no more water than clings to it from washing. Purée it in an electric blender and heat it again to evaporate any remaining water. Knead it into the dough after the eggs are incorporated. Proceed as for plain *lasagne,* letting them dry on cloths for about an hour before using. Use to make baked green *lasagne bolognese* (*see* Index). Or, cut the sheets of dough into ¼-inch strips to make green noodles, and serve with butter and grated Parmesan or any desired sauce.

CATHEDRAL AND BAPTISTRY—CREMONA   *Lombardy*

Stuffed Tomatoes
Pomidori Ripieni

(Tomatoes, tuna fish, capers, anchovies, parsley, mayonnaise, egg, pickle)

Cut 2 large tomatoes in half, shake out seeds and liquid, and hollow the centers slightly. Fill them with diced tuna fish mixed with a small teaspoon of Italian salted capers, first rinsed and dried, 2 anchovy fillets, cut in small pieces, minced parsley, and mayonnaise flavored with mustard. Place a slice of hard-boiled egg on each tomato half, and top each one with a slice of small sour gherkin. Serves four as a first course.

FOUNTAIN IN THE PAPAL PALACE—VITERBO   *Latium*

Hot Cauliflower Salad

Insalata di Cavolfiore Calda

(Cauliflower, olive oil, garlic, mustard, wine vinegar, parsley)

Trim a firm white cauliflower and soak it in cold water for half an hour. Divide it into flowerettes. Cook these in boiling salted water not quite to cover, taking care not to overcook or break the pieces. Drain them well and reassemble them in the semblance of a whole cauliflower. Meanwhile, heat 6 tablespoons of olive oil, and in it steep 1 minced clove of garlic over low heat, being careful not to brown the garlic. Stir in ½ teaspoon of mixed mustard, 2 tablespoons of wine vinegar, salt and pepper, and 1 teaspoon of finely minced parsley. Blend the dressing well, reheat it, and pour it over the cauliflower. This salad may also be served cold. In this case do not heat the dressing. Serves four.

PIAZZA DANTE — VERONA   *Veneto*

Baked Onions in White Wine
Cipolle al Vino Bianco
(Onions, parsley, basil, white wine, butter)

Cover 1½ pounds of white boiling onions, unpeeled, with cold water. Bring the water to a boil and cook the onions for 12 minutes. Peel them and place them in a baking dish or small casserole with 1 tablespoon of chopped parsley and 2 teaspoons of chopped fresh basil (or 1 teaspoon of dried basil). Add ¾ cup of dry white wine, salt and pepper, and 1 teaspoon of sugar, and dot with 3 tablespoons of butter. Cover the dish closely and bake the onions in a 300° oven for 1 hour, or until they are tender and the liquid is almost absorbed; remove the cover for the last 20 minutes if necessary to reduce the juices. Serves four.

PONTREMOLI   *Tuscany*

Chicken Livornese

Pollo alla Livornese

(Chicken, butter, lemon, olive oil, parsley, chicken broth)

Wipe a 3½-pound roasting chicken inside and out with a damp cloth. Salt it inside, place a tablespoon of butter and a slice of lemon in the cavity, and truss it. Use a heavy deep pan or casserole with a tightly fitting lid from which steam cannot escape later. First brown the chicken lightly in the casserole in 2 tablespoons of olive oil. When it is pale gold on all sides, add ¼ cup of chicken broth, the juice of 1 lemon, and ½ teaspoon of chopped parsley. Cover the casserole, place it on an asbestos mat over a very low fire, and cook the chicken for about 1¾ to 2 hours or until it is tender; it is steamed rather than roasted. Serve it with small buttered and parsleyed new potatoes. Serves four to six.

BIRD'S-EYE VIEW OF VIBTRI   *Campania*

Spaghetti Neapolitan
Spaghetti alla Napolitana

(Oil, garlic, onion, ham, sausage, stock, Tomato Sauce, spaghetti)

Heat 3 tablespoons of olive oil in a saucepan, and add 2 chopped and mashed cloves of garlic and 1 small chopped onion. Cook them slowly until they are pale gold, then add 3 tablespoons of finely chopped ham and ½ pound of fresh Italian sausage, peeled and chopped. Let these cook together for 3 or 4 minutes, then add 1 cup of hot meat stock or bouillon and 1 cup of Tomato Sauce (either canned or homemade). Cover the pan and simmer the sauce very slowly for 10 to 15 minutes, or until it is of the desired consistency. This makes enough sauce for 1 pound of spaghetti, to serve six. Pour the sauce over the freshly cooked spaghetti, sprinkle with grated Parmesan cheese, and serve at once.

FARMYARD IN THE HILLS   *Tuscany*

Artichokes Florentine
Carciofi alla Fiorentina

(Artichoke bases, cauliflower, mushrooms, butter, flour, milk, nutmeg, cheese)

Use the bases of 8 boiled artichokes, with leaves and chokes removed, or large canned artichoke bases. Divide a small cauliflower into flowerettes and boil them in salted water until cooked but not too soft. Clean and dice ½ pound of mushrooms, and cook them in 2½ tablespoons of hot butter for about 5 minutes, or until all liquid has evaporated. Make a bechamel sauce by blending 1 tablespoon of flour into 1 tablespoon of melted butter and adding gradually 1 cup of rich milk or thin cream. Stir continually, and add salt and pepper and a dash of nutmeg. When the sauce is thickened and perfectly smooth, add 3 tablespoons of grated Swiss or Parmesan cheese. Arrange the artichoke bases in a shallow buttered baking dish, place the mushrooms on them and then the cauliflower pieces. Spoon some of the sauce over each one, and sprinkle them with a little grated Parmesan cheese. Bake in a 400° oven for about 10 minutes, or until the tops are lightly browned. Serves eight.

123

THE HARBOR AT NERVI *Liguria*

Poached Fish with Green Sauce
Pesce alla Salsa Verde

(Fish, white wine, onion, carrot, parsley, bay leaf, lemon, olive oil)

This basic recipe may be used for poaching any type of fish: Combine 2 cups each of water and white wine, and add a few slices each of onion and carrot, parsley, a bay leaf, a slice of lemon, salt and pepper, and 3 tablespoons of olive oil. Simmer this *court-bouillon*, covered, for 20 minutes. Wrap a thick 3-pound piece of fish in cheese cloth or a fine muslin, place it in the broth, and poach it at a very low simmer for about 25 minutes. It is done when it feels firm when pressed with a finger; the timing depends on the thickness of the piece of fish. Remove it from the broth, unwrap it, let it drain a little, and place it on a hot platter. Remove all the skin and decorate the platter with parsley and lemon slices. Serve with Green Sauce (*see* Index). Serves six.

124

CETARA   *Campania*

Mozzarella "in a Coach"

Mozzarella in Carrozza

(Bread, Mozzarella cheese, eggs, bread crumbs, oil)

This is an Italian form of "cheese dream" or fried cheese sandwich: Trim the crust from sixteen ¼-inch-thick slices of bread and cut them into halves or quarters. Cut 16 or 32 slices of all-cream Mozzarella slightly smaller than the slices of bread, and assemble the sandwiches, pressing the edges together. Beat together 2 eggs, ¼ teaspoon of salt, and a teaspoon of water. Dip the sandwiches in this, coating both sides and all the edges well. Let them stand to become well impregnated, then dip the edges in fine bread crumbs to seal them as much as possible. Fry the sandwiches, a few at a time, to a fine golden color in hot oil almost 1 inch deep in a small frying pan, turning them to brown on each side. Drain them on absorbent paper and serve immediately on a hot plate.

125

THE COLUMNS OF THE FORUM—POMPEI   *Campania*

Dried Beef Antipasto
Bresaola
(Dried beef, olive oil, lemon, parsley)

Spread out thin slices of dried or chipped beef, brush them well with olive oil, and sprinkle them with lemon juice and finely chopped parsley. Let them marinate for several hours. To serve, arrange the slices overlapping in rows on a platter, or roll each slice and line up the little rolls in rows. Pour the remaining marinade over them. Serve as one of a variety of *antipasti*.

THE CHURCH AT CANNERO *Piedmont*

Veal Cutlets Parmesan
Scaloppine di Vitello alla Parmigiana
(Veal cutlets, butter, Mozzarella, Tomato Sauce, Parmesan)

Between sheets of waxed paper pound 8 small veal cutlets to less than ¼-inch thickness. Pounded, they should be about the size of the palm of your hand. Dry them well, dip them lightly in flour, and season them with salt and pepper. Sauté them over a brisk fire in 4 tablespoons of hot butter; they should be brown enough after 2 to 3 minutes of cooking on each side. Arrange the *scaloppine* in one layer in a flameproof dish. Place a thin slice of Mozzarella cheese on each cutlet, and put them under the broiler until the cheese melts. Meanwhile, to the pan in which the veal was cooked add 1½ cups of Tomato Sauce (either canned or homemade) and heat it well, stirring in the brown juices in the pan. Spoon this sauce over the cutlets, and sprinkle it with grated Parmesan. Serve at once, in the same dish. Serves four.

127

POMPEI   *Campania*

Mushrooms in Oil
Funghi sotto Olio

(Mushrooms, garlic, onion, bay leaves, vinegar, peppercorns, cloves, olive oil)

Trim the tips of the stems of 2 pounds of button mushrooms and rinse them in salted water. Drain them, and put them in an enameled saucepan with 1 teaspoon of salt, 2 cloves of garlic, 1 onion, and 2 bay leaves. Combine 3 cups each of water and white-wine vinegar, bring to a boil, and pour over the mushrooms. Bring the liquid back to a boil, then cook the mushrooms for 5 minutes. Drain and cool, discarding the garlic, onion, and bay leaves. Put the mushrooms in 2 sterilized 1-pint jars, adding to each jar 1 bay leaf, 6 peppercorns, and 2 cloves; use a wooden spoon to pack the mushrooms in the jars, taking care not to damage them. Then fill the jars to the brim with olive oil, seal them, and keep them in a cool place for a month or more before using. These are excellent in a dish of assorted *antipasti*.

THE CATHEDRAL CLOISTER — MONREALE   *Sicily*

Roast Stuffed Partridge
Pernice Arrosto

(Partridge, celery, olive oil, white wine, herbs, bread crumbs, egg, bacon, stock)

This recipe is for a 2½-pound partridge but may also be used for a small chicken: Sauté 1 chopped celery stalk (about ¼ cup) and the chopped liver of the partridge for 5 minutes in 2 tablespoons of olive oil. Add ⅓ cup of white wine, salt, pepper, 2 teaspoons each of minced chives and parsley, and a pinch of orégano. Combine this mixture with 1½ cups of stale bread torn into coarse crumbs, 1 small lightly beaten egg, and mix all together lightly. Stuff the partridge, truss it, and tie strips of bacon over the breast. Roast it in a 325° oven for about 1 hour or until done; remove the bacon for the last 10 minutes to brown the bird. Transfer the partridge to a hot platter. Skim the fat from the surface of the pan juices, stir in a small amount of strong stock, reheat on top of the stove, and serve in a sauceboat. Serves two.

VIA DEI MONTI   *Rome*

Fettuccine with Anchovies

Fettuccine alla Romana

(Egg noodles, butter, anchovies)

In a large kettle of salted water boil 1 pound of narrow egg noodles (either the packaged kind or Homemade *Pasta*) until just tender but still firm. Meanwhile let 6 tablespoons of unsalted butter soften at room temperature. Mash 6 anchovy fillets to a paste and cream them thoroughly into the butter. Drain the *fettuccine*, mix them well with the seasoned butter, and serve immediately. Serves six.

130

LAKE COMO   *Lombardy*

Pot Roast alla Certosina

Manzo alla Certosina

(Round of beef, oil, butter, bacon, anchovies, nutmeg, parsley, stock)

In a heavy pot heat together 1 tablespoon each of olive oil and butter. Put in a 2½-pound piece of rump or round of beef; the eye of the round is a good piece for this dish. Add 2 slices of bacon, cut in pieces, and brown the beef on all sides. Then add 3 chopped anchovy fillets, pepper, a small pinch of salt, a pinch of nutmeg, 2 teaspoons of chopped parsley, and 1 cup of hot stock. Cover the pot and simmer the beef slowly for about 2 hours, more or less; this will depend on the cut of beef you use. Add more stock or water to the pot while the beef is cooking if the juices become too reduced. When it is tender, remove the meat to a hot platter and slice it. Strain the sauce, skim off most of the fat, and pour the sauce over the meat. Serves six.

131

VENICE   *Veneto*

Marzipan-Stuffed Apricots
Albicocche Marzapane
(Dried apricots, almond paste, sugar, egg white)

Wash 1 pound of large dried apricots and soak them in cold water for an hour. Drain them and place them in saucepan with enough cold water to cover. Heat them slowly to the boiling point; they should be cooked just until tender and not too soft. Drain and cool them, and pat them dry.

Cut into small pieces the contents of an 8-ounce can of unsweetened almond paste. Mix this thoroughly with 1 cup plus 2 tablespoons of granulated sugar. Add the white of 1 small egg, first beaten to a froth, and work the paste until no lumps remain. Fill each apricot with some of the almond paste, then roll them in plenty of granulated sugar. Spread them out on a board or platter, and let them dry in a cool place for 12 hours.

132

FARMHOUSE NEAR ORTISEI   *Trentino-Alto Adige*

Italian Meat Balls
Polpette
(Ground beef, parsley, garlic, lemon rind, nutmeg, bread crumbs, egg)

To 1 pound of lean ground beef add a mixture of 2 teaspoons of minced parsley, 1 small minced and crushed clove of garlic, and the grated zest of 1 small lemon. Add salt and pepper, a dash of grated nutmeg, 3 tablespoons of dry bread crumbs, and 1 beaten egg. Mix all lightly together, shape into cakes, and cook these slowly for 2 or 3 minutes on each side in hot butter or olive oil. Serves four.

133

COUNTRY ROAD NEAR LUCCA   *Tuscany*

Italian Rice Tuscany
Risotto alla Toscana

(Italian Rice, Tomato Sauce, salami, butter, Parmesan)

Make a *risotto* (Italian Rice; *see* Index). To the 3½ cups of broth needed for the 1 cup of rice add 3 tablespoons of Tomato Sauce. When the rice is done, stir in ¼ pound of good imported salami, sliced rather thick, skinned, and cut in small dice. Add ¼ cup of grated Parmesan cheese and a lump of butter, and cover the *risotto* until it is served. Serves four.

THE CATHEDRAL AT LUCCA   *Tuscany*

Roast Beef Leghorn

Arrosto di Manzo Livornese

(Sirloin roast, ham or bacon, cloves, red wine, butter, onion)

Have a 5- to 6-pound sirloin roast boned and tied. Along the top, with a sharp knife, make two rows of small slits; into each one insert a strip of ham or lean bacon. (The way to do this is to poke in the ham or bacon while the knife is still in the meat; then pull out the knife, holding in the little piece of ham as you pull.) Insert also a dozen cloves here and there in the meat. Place the roast in an oval enamelled casserole or bowl just large enough to hold it, and pour over it 1 cup of good red wine. Let the meat marinate, covered, overnight. Then remove it from the marinade, wipe it dry, place it in a roasting pan, and dot it with butter. Start roasting it according to your taste (about 18 minutes per pound in a 325° oven for rare beef). Meanwhile sauté 1 chopped onion in butter until it is soft but not brown, and add this to the roast; and from time to time add some of the marinade and baste the meat with this. Serve the pan juices in a sauceboat with the beef. Serves eight.

135

PASSO DI SELLA   *Trentino-Alto Adige*

Mixed Boiled Meats
Il Bollito Misto

(Fowl, veal knuckle, beef, sausage, vegetables, Green Sauce)

The original of this great dish from northern Italy is frightening in the size and number of its ingredients (including a calf's head), but it can be made on a manageable scale: To a large kettle of boiling water add a trussed boiling fowl or capon; a knuckle of veal; 2½ pounds of lean beef (chuck, round, or boned rolled breast); and a large Italian pork boiling sausage (in Italy called *cotechino*). Put these in in sequence according to estimated cooking times; the knuckle of veal for the full time; 2½ hours for the fowl (2 hours for capon); 2 to 3 hours for the beef (this depends on the cut); and the time specified on the wrappings for the sausage. The ingredients should be half to three quarters covered by the boiling water, which should be kept at a low simmer throughout; add 2 teaspoons of salt after the first hour. Test the fowl with a fork for real tenderness, the beef for somewhat firm tenderness; if one is done before the other, remove it and return it to the hot stock briefly before serving. Serve the meats, carved, on a hot platter, moistened with stock (this is, of course, a flavorful soup besides). Serve also boiled potatoes, onions, and cabbage. *Salsa verde* (Green Sauce; *see* Index) is indispensable with this dish; mustard is also usual. You have enough meat for eight or more and it is good cold with the same sauce.

136

CEFALÙ   *Sicily*

Chicken with Mushrooms
Pollo ai Funghi
(Chicken, butter, olive oil, garlic, onion, mushrooms, white wine, tomato sauce)

Cut a 3-pound broiling chicken into serving pieces, season them lightly with salt and pepper, and dust them with flour. Brown them slowly, for about 5 minutes on each side, in 2 tablespoons each of heated butter and olive oil. Add a peeled cut clove of garlic midway in the browning process; when the chicken is browned, remove the garlic. Then add 1 chopped onion and ½-pound of mushrooms, cleaned and quartered. Stir them in and cook all together for 5 or 6 minutes. Add ½ cup of dry white wine and salt and pepper, cover the pan, and cook the chicken slowly until the liquid is half evaporated. Add 3 tablespoons of tomato sauce and 2 tablespoons of water, cover the pan again, and cook the chicken on a very low fire until it is done, or for about 15 to 20 minutes. A few minutes before it is done, sprinkle it with 1 teaspoon of finely minced parsley. Serves four.

137

CHURCH OF SAN GIOVANNI—SIRACUSA   *Sicily*

Sicilian Baked Fish
Trance di Pesce alla Siciliana

(Fresh swordfish or tuna, olive oil, parsley, garlic, vinegar, tomatoes, peas)

The original of this recipe calls for *palamita*, or *bonito*, which is a kind of small tuna fish. It is an excellent way to prepare any firm-textured fish, particularly swordfish. To serve four, use 4 slices of fish totalling about 2 pounds. Dip them lightly in flour. In an earthern or enamelled casserole brown the slices lightly on each side in ⅜ cup of hot olive oil; when you turn the slices, add 1 tablespoon of chopped parsley and 1 finely chopped clove of garlic. When the fish is browned, add ½ cup of white-wine vinegar, and simmer until this is practically evaporated. Then add 4 medium-large tomatoes, peeled, seeded, and coarsely chopped. Bring to a simmer and then cook for another 5 minutes. Shell in advance 2 pounds of green peas, and add these now to the dish. Season with salt and pepper, and cook all together, covered, for about 30 minutes. Serve with Italian bread either toasted or fried in oil. Serves four.

138

THE PORT OF BOCCADASSE—GENOA   *Liguria*

Baked Tomatoes Genoa Style

Pomidori Genovese

(Tomatoes, olive oil, garlic, marjoram, parsley, Parmesan)

Cut 4 firm, ripe tomatoes in half and shake out the seeds. Place the tomatoes in an oiled baking dish, cut sides up, and pour 2 teaspoons of olive oil into each half. Sprinkle them with finely chopped garlic, with chopped fresh marjoram and parsley in equal quantities, and with salt and pepper and a good coating of grated Parmesan. Bake them in a 350° oven for about 15 minutes, or until they are lightly browned and moderately soft and the flavors are well blended. Serves four.

PERUGIA   *Umbria*

Green-Pepper Omelette

Frittata con Peperoni

(Green peppers, olive oil, garlic, eggs)

Clean 2 sweet green peppers, removing all the seeds and inside ribs. Slice them into thin strips about an inch long. In a frying pan heat 4 tablespoons of olive oil, add the peppers, and let them cook over gentle heat for about 15 minutes, or until softened and lightly browned. Five minutes before they are done, add 1 small clove of garlic, chopped and mashed. Beat 5 eggs with a little salt and pepper and pour them over the peppers. Stir all well together and let the mixture cook until the eggs are firm. Serve at once. This omelette is not turned over as is a true *frittata*. Serves three or four.

WHEAT AND OXEN — CASTEL *Marche*

Homemade Pasta

Pasta

(Flour, salt, eggs, water)

A rolling-and-cutting machine is a big help in making *pasta,* but the flavor of the real homemade thing is worth the work even without a machine: Into a large bowl sift together 4 cups of flour and 2 teaspoons of salt. Make a well in the center and pour 3 lightly beaten eggs into it. Mix flour and eggs gradually with one hand, adding a little at a time about ¼ cup of water, or just enough to make a firm dough barely soft enough to handle. Then knead it on a floured board for a good 12 minutes; it must be elastic and perfectly smooth. Divide it into four parts to make it easier to handle, and roll out the pieces one at a time on a large floured board. Stretch the dough with the rolling pin until it is between ¹⁄₁₆ and ⅛ of an inch thick; sprinkle it with flour and flour the rolling pin as needed. Roll up each sheet of paste loosely for cutting: For noodles *(tagliatelle or fettuccine),* slice the rolls in widths of about ¼ inch; for *lasagne,* cut them into strips 1½ inches wide and cut the strips into 5-inch lengths. Spread the cut *pasta* on cloths on table tops to dry for about an hour before cooking. Then boil them for 5 minutes in salted water, drain, and serve with butter, and with grated Parmesan if desired, or with a sauce *(see* Index). Makes about 1 pound of *pasta,* or enough to serve six.

THE BORDER TOWN OF VINTIMIGLIA   *Liguria*

Smoked Salmon Antipasto

Antipasto di Salmone Affumicato

(Smoked salmon, butter, anchovies, shallot)

In a small mortar or bowl pound and rub a few fillets of anchovy to a smooth paste. Mix them with sweet, unsalted butter and a small amount of finely chopped shallot. Spread this flavored butter on thin slices of smoked salmon. The amount of anchovy and shallot is a matter of taste, but remember that the salmon, too, is salty, as well as the anchovy. The slices may be rolled and served as one of an assortment of *antipasti,* or they may be cut into small sections and served on toast as cocktail hors-d'oeuvre. Chill before serving.

THE ALPS   *Valle d'Aosta*

Filets Mignons
Filettini

(Beef tenderloin steaks, oil, butter, anchovy paste, croutons, mushrooms, Marsala)

Have 6 filets mignons (steaks from the center of the tenderloin) each tied around with string. Cut 6 slices of bread less than ½ inch thick from a round Italian loaf, and trim off the crusts; they should be about the size and shape of the tenderloin steaks. Cut a circle in the center of each slice, not too deep and about ⅜ of an inch from the edge all around. Fry the bread on both sides in a mixture of oil and butter. Then remove the top layer of the circle cut in each crouton, and keep them warm. Cream 2½ tablespoons of butter with a little anchovy paste, melt this in a large hot skillet, and in it brown the filets mignons on both sides, rather slowly, until they are well browned but still quite rare in the center.

Meanwhile broil or sauté 6 mushroom caps in a little butter. Spread the hollowed centers of each crouton with butter, place a filet mignon on each, remove the strings, and top with the mushroom caps. Add about ⅜ cup of Marsala to the juices in the skillet, heat, stir, and simmer briefly, and spoon this sauce over the filets. Serves six.

SAN FRANCESCO DI PAOLA — NAPLES   *Campania*

Green Lasagne Bolognese

Lasagne Verdi Bolognese

(Green lasagne, bolognose meat sauce, butter, flour, milk, cream, Parmesan)

First make *bolognese* meat sauce (*see* Index). Then make homemade green *lasagne (see* Index); use about half of it to serve six to eight, and save the rest for another day (they keep well when dried). Cook the *lasagne,* two or three at a time, for 3 minutes in a large kettle of boiling salted water. With a large spoon, remove each one as it is done and drop it into a bowl of cold water. Then place them in a single layer on damp towels to drain.

Make a rich cream sauce by blending 3 tablespoons of flour into 3 tablespoons of melted butter and adding gradually 1 cup each of milk and cream. Season the sauce with salt and pepper, and stir it with a whisk until it is smooth and thickened. Spread a little *bolognese* meat sauce in a shallow oblong buttered baking dish. Spoon a little cream sauce over it, and then sprinkle the cream sauce with grated Parmesan cheese. Over this place carefully a layer of the boiled *lasagne,* allowing the ends to turn partly up the sides at the two ends of the dish. Repeat these layers until the dish is almost full, ending with a generous layer of meat sauce, then more cream sauce and Parmesan. The dish is best when composed of many thin layers with plenty of sauce on top. Bake it in a 375° oven for about 25 minutes, or until the *lasagne* shrink a little away from the sides of the dish.

144

CHURCH OF SANTA GIUSTINA—PADUA   *Veneto Euganea*

Fried Stuffed Crepes
Crepes Fritte Imbottite

(Crepe Batter, tongue, Swiss cheese, white truffles or mushrooms, butter)

To serve four, make one recipe of Crepe Batter (*see* Index) and let it rest for 2 hours in the refrigerator. Make the 8 crepes and spread them out on a board. Place a thin slice of tongue on each one, and on this spread several thin, narrow strips of Swiss cheese. In the center of each arrange several slices of white Italian truffle or, lacking these, a few slices of cooked mushrooms. Roll the crepes rather closely, turning in the open ends before the rolls are quite completed to make a closed package of each. Roll them lightly in flour, and fry them quickly in a generous amount of hot butter until they are slightly crisp. Serve at once.

DRY DOCK—CETARA *Campania*

Roast Lamb with Anchovy Sauce
Abbachio in Salsa d'Acciughe

(Leg of lamb, garlic, ginger, white wine, stock, anchovies, parsley, lemon rind)

Remove most of the fat from a leg of young spring lamb. Insert 4 or 5 cut sections of garlic near the bone and in the meat here and there. Rub a little salt, pepper, and powdered ginger into the surface of the meat. Roast the lamb in a 350° oven for 13 minutes per pound. Baste it with the pan juices to which you add from time to time a little white wine and stock. When the lamb is done but still pink in the center, remove it to a hot platter. To the juices in the roasting pan add 6 chopped anchovy fillets and stir until they dissolve. Add 2 teaspoons of finely chopped parsley and 1 teaspoon of grated lemon rind, reheat the sauce, and pass it in a sauceboat.

146

VENICE   *Veneto*

Venetian Fried Cream
Crema Fritta alla Veneziana

(Egg yolks, sugar, flour, milk, salt, bread crumbs, oil)

For each serving: Beat together 1 egg yolk and 1 tablespoon of sugar, blend in smoothly 1 tablespoon of flour, add gradually ¾ cup of milk, and add a pinch of salt. Cook the cream for 45 minutes over simmering water, stirring often. Then spread the cream out on a baking sheet in a layer less than ½ inch thick, and let it cool. Cut the cream into lozenge shapes or squares, and dip these in beaten egg and then in fine bread crumbs. In a skillet fry them in hot oil ½ inch deep, turning them once, until they are golden brown on both sides. Drain them, sprinkle with sugar, and serve at once.

SPOLETO   *Umbria*

Steak Hunter Style

Bistecca alla Cacciatora

(Steak, oil, garlic, fennel seeds, red wine, Marsala, tomato, parsley)

Heat 1 tablespoon of olive oil in a heavy iron skillet, and in it panbroil a thick steak for two, browning each side well and removing it to a hot platter when it is cooked but still rare in the center. Remove some of the fat in the pan, leaving about 2 teaspoons. Add 1 minced clove of garlic, ½ teaspoon of fennel seeds, ½ cup of red wine, and 2 tablespoons of Marsala. Stir up the brown juices in the pan, and let the wine boil until it is reduced to about ¼ cup. Then add 1 rather small tomato, peeled, seeded, and chopped, and salt and pepper. Simmer the sauce for 2 or 3 minutes, add 1 teaspoon of minced parsley, pour it over the steak, and serve at once.

ON THE BEACH AT SESTRI LEVANTE *Liguria*

Fish Soup with Tomatoes
Zuppa di Pesce con Pomidori

(Fish, olive oil, onion, garlic, celery, green pepper, tomatoes, orègano)

Use 2 pounds of fish fillets of your choice, which may include haddock or cod, sole, mullet, mackerel, whiting, or whatever fresh fish you can get that is fairly firm in texture. Use a combination of two or three types if possible, as this seems to add flavor to the soup.

Heat ⅜ cup of olive oil in a deep saucepan, and in this cook slowly 1 onion and 1 clove of garlic, both minced, 1 stalk of celery with some of its leaves, finely chopped, and ½ a green pepper, sliced and chopped. When the vegetables have softened a little, add 2 pounds of ripe tomatoes, peeled and coarsely chopped (or the equivalent in canned Italian tomatoes). Add salt and pepper and ½ teaspoon of orègano. Boil the mixture briskly for 5 minutes, then cover the pan, lower the heat, and simmer the soup slowly for 15 minutes. Now add the fish, cut in rather large sections, and at this point add a little hot water if it seems necessary; the soup should be rather thick, more like a stew than a soup. Cover the pan and cook for about 15 minutes or until the fish is tender. Serve with Italian bread or with croutons rubbed with garlic and fried in oil. Serves six.

FARMHOUSE NEAR PISTOIA   *Tuscany*

Baked Lasagne
Lasagne al Forno

(Lasagne, Tomato Sauce, Parmesan, Mozzarella)

If you use Homemade *Pasta* for this dish, make 1 pound, roll it thin, and cut it in pieces 1½ inches wide and 5 inches long. Boil these *lasagne,* a few at a time, for 5 minutes in a large quantity of salted water. Lift them out as they are done, drop them into cold water to cool, then spread them on cloths to dry. Bought, dried *lasagne* require a longer cooking time.

Line a buttered baking dish with the *lasagne.* Cover them with homemade Tomato Sauce *(see* Index) or a good canned variety, and cover this with grated Parmesan and a layer of thinly sliced Mozzarella. Repeat the layers until you have used all the *pasta,* finishing with a layer of sauce and grated cheese. Bake the dish in a 350° oven for about 20 minutes, or until it is bubbling hot. Serves six.

RENAISSANCE STAIRCASE—VERONA   *Veneto*

Asparagus Mold
Sformato di Asparagi

(Asparagus, butter, flour, milk, nutmeg, Parmesan, eggs, croutons, cream sauce)

A *sformato* is a "formed" or molded dish. It somewhat resembles a timbale, being not quite a soufflé nor yet a pudding. A *sformato* makes a delectable small entrée or luncheon dish and is easier to handle than a soufflé.

Cut the tender tips from 4 pounds of asparagus, boil these in salted water for 10 minutes, or until just done, drain them, and cut them into small pieces. Make a thick cream sauce by blending 4 tablespoons of flour into 3 tablespoons of melted butter and adding gradually 1¼ cups of milk. Season the sauce with salt, pepper, and a dash of nutmeg. Let it cool a little, then stir in 2 tablespoons of grated Parmesan, 3 large well-beaten eggs, and the asparagus tips. Butter a mold or soufflé dish, coat it lightly with fine bread crumbs, and pour in the mixture to fill the dish by about two thirds. Cover it with a buttered paper, stand it in a pan of hot water, and cook it in a 325° oven for 40 minutes to 1 hour, or until a thin skewer or a knife inserted into the center of the dish comes out clean. Turn the *sformato* out onto a hot platter, surround it with triangular croutons of bread fried crisp in butter, and serve it with a medium-thick cream sauce made with thin cream instead of milk. Serves six.

151

RIVELLO   *Calabria*

Calabrian Turnovers
Pitte con Niepita

(Grape jam, sugar, cinnamon, walnuts, cocoa, rum, pastry dough, egg yolk)

The distinctive thing about these little turnovers is the unusual flavor of the filling. The base is grape jam which must be quite firm. If necessary, thicken 1 cup of grape jam by melting it over low heat and stirring into it 2 or 3 teaspoons of potato starch first dissolved in a few drops of cold water. Let it cool. Add ¼ cup of sugar, ⅛ teaspoon of cinnamon, ½ cup of ground walnut meats, 6 table-spoons of cocoa, and 1 tablespoon of rum. Make a pie dough, or use a good mix, sweetened with a little sugar. Roll it out rather thin, cut it into 3½-inch rounds, and put a spoonful of filling in the center of each round. Moisten the edges of the dough, turn the rounds over in half over their filling, and pinch the edges together. Prick the tops of the turnovers with the tip of a pointed knife, and brush them with egg yolk. Bake them on a floured baking sheet in a 400° oven for 15 minutes. Serve hot or cold.

ANCIENT HILLSIDE   *Tuscany*

Chicken Breasts Modena

Filetti di Pollo alla Modenese

(Chicken breasts, egg, bread crumbs, butter, oil, Canadian bacon, Fontina cheese)

Bone and skin 2 pairs of chicken breasts. Slice the meat horizontally, as thinly as possible, in order to obtain 8 wide thin slices. Pound these lightly between sheets of waxed paper, and trim them to even shapes. Dip the slices lightly in seasoned flour, then in egg beaten with a few drops of water, and then in fine bread crumbs. Heat together 6 tablespoons of butter and 4 tablespoons of olive oil. When the fat is very hot but not brown, add the chicken breasts, and cook them for 3 or 4 minutes on each side, or until they are golden brown. Butter a shallow baking dish, arrange in it, in one layer, 8 slices of Canadian bacon, and on these place thin slices of Fontina or Swiss cheese. Over the cheese place the chicken breasts, and then another layer of slices of Canadian bacon and cheese. Bake the dish in a 400° oven until the cheese is melted. Serve with tiny buttered green beans or peas. Serves four or six.

153

VILLA CIMBRONE—RAVELLO   *Campania*

Shirred Eggs with Prosciutto and Mozzarella
Uova con Prosciutto e Mozzarella

(Eggs, prosciutto or ham, Mozzarella cheese, butter)

Butter a shallow baking dish large enough to hold 6 eggs, or use 6 individual shirred-egg dishes. On the bottom place 6 slices of *prosciutto* (smoked raw Italian ham) or of thinly sliced baked ham. Cover these with thin slices of Mozzarella cheese. Break 6 eggs carefully into the dish, leaving spaces between them. Salt and pepper them lightly, and place ½ teaspoon of butter on each egg. Bake them in a 400° oven until the eggs are set and the cheese is melted. Serves six.

154

THE HARVESTERS *Calabria*

Pork Chops with Vinegar
Maiale all'Aceto
(Pork chops, butter, white-wine vinegar, anchovies)

Remove the fat from 6 boned loin pork chops, and pound them thin. In a large skillet, brown them on each side in 3 tablespoons of butter. Then drain off most of the fat, and add salt and pepper, ¾ cup of white-wine vinegar, and ¼ cup of water. Cook the chops, covered, for about 30 minutes, or until they are tender. Add a little hot stock to the pan if necessary during the cooking. Remove the chops to a hot platter. To the pan juices add 4 chopped anchovy fillets, stir until they have dissolved, and blend in 2 teaspoons of butter first worked to a paste with ½ teaspoon of flour. Reheat the sauce until it is well blended and slightly thickened; there should not be too much of it. Pour the sauce over the chops, and serve with fluffy mashed potatoes or fried apples. Serves six.

155

ROMAN AMPHITHEATRE—TRIESTE *Friuli-Venezia Giulia*

Wild Duck with Marsala Sauce
Anitra Selvatica

(Wild duck, butter, olive oil, parsley, garlic, orange, Marsala)

Rub a drawn wild duck with butter. Preheat the oven to 500°, put the duck in a roasting pan, and when you put it in the oven, lower the heat to 350°. While the duck is roasting, baste it often with the following sauce: Heat together in a small saucepan 2 tablespoons of olive oil, 1 teaspoon of minced parsley, 1 small clove of garlic, chopped and mashed, and salt and pepper. When the mixture is hot, add ¼ cup of Marsala, 2 tablespoons of stock, and the juice and grated rind of 1 orange. Turn the heat very low, and keep the sauce hot but not boiling as you baste the duck with it. After about 30 minutes, the duck should be done to the rare but not raw stage. Remove it to a hot platter. Deglaze the roasting pan with the remainder of the sauce if you have any left, add another spoonful of Marsala, and pass this sauce separately. Serves two.

VILLAGE IN THE FOOTHILLS   *Umbria*

Fricassee of New Carrots
Fricassea di Carote Novelle
(Carrots, butter, ham, parsley)

Wash and scrape 2 dozen or more tiny new carrots. Heat 2 or 3 tablespoons of butter in a broad saucepan, add the carrots, salt and pepper them, and cook them slowly over low heat, stirring often, until they are tender. If small tender carrots are not available, use larger ones cut in pieces and shaped with a knife into rounded or oval pieces. Parboil them for 8 minutes in boiling salted water, drain them well, and proceed as above. When the carrots are done, add ½ cup of finely diced cooked ham, stir and reheat the mixture, and sprinkle with minced parsley. Serves four.

MARKET AT SAN REMO   *Liguria*

Clear Soup with Garden Custard Drops
Brodo con Rombetti alla Giardiniera

(Peas, carrot, spinach, parsley, eggs, Parmesan, Italian Broth or consommé)

Boil separately until tender ½ cup of peas, 1 small sliced carrot, and a couple of handfuls of spinach leaves. Drain them well; press all the water from the spinach, chop it, and drain it again. Force the vegetables through a fine sieve, and add 2 teaspoons of very finely minced parsley. Beat 3 eggs, and add to them 3 tablespoons of grated Parmesan and the strained vegetables. Stir the ingredients well together, and pour this custard into a buttered glass pie dish. Stand the dish in a shallow pan of hot water, and bake the custard in a 325° oven until it is firm. Let it cool, turn it out on a plate, and cut it into small lozenge shapes. Put a few of these in each soup plate before pouring in boiling hot Italian Broth or clear consommé.

CHURCH AT CHIARI   *Piedmont*

Baked Lasagne Piedmontese

Lasagne al Forno Piemontese

(Lasagne, Parmesan, Mozzarella, onion, mushrooms, sausage, tomatoes, Ricotta)

Butter a shallow rectangular baking dish and line it with a layer of cooked *lasagne* (*see* Index); have the *pasta* extend up the sides and over the edge at the two ends of the dish. Spread a layer of sauce (*see* below) over the *lasagne*, sprinkle it with grated Parmesan, and cover this completely with a layer of thin slices of Mozzarella. Now spread on another layer of *lasagne*, this time without allowing the ends to extend up the sides of the dish. Add more sauce and grated cheese, and repeat until all the ingredients are used, finishing with a layer of sauce and Parmesan. Fold the extended ends of *pasta* back over the top at the ends of the dish. Bake in a 350° oven for about 25 minutes, or until the *lasagne* shrinks a little away from the sides of the dish.

Piemontese sauce: Chop 1 large onion and cook it slowly in 2 tablespoons of hot butter and 1 tablespoon of olive oil until it is soft and beginning to brown. Add ¼ pound of chopped mushrooms and ¼ pound of fresh Italian sausage, peeled and chopped, and cook the mixture slowly for about 6 minutes. Add 1 pound of peeled and chopped tomatoes, salt and pepper to taste, and simmer the sauce for about 30 minutes. Just before assembling the dish, stir into the sauce ¼ pound of crumbled Ricotta cheese. Serves six.

159

HOUSE ACROSS THE TIBER　　　　　　　　　　　　　　*Rome*

Noodles Trasteverina

Tagliatelle alla Trasteverina

(Noodles, butter, Parmesan, onion, bacon, chicken giblets, wine, Tomato Sauce)

Boil in salted water 1 pound of noodles (or Homemade *Pasta*) such as *tagliatelle* or *fettuccine*. Drain them while they are still somewhat firm, mix in some softened butter, place them in a serving dish, and serve them with the following sauce poured into the center and sprinkled generously with grated Parmesan or Pecorino cheese.

Chop 1 onion and cook it slowly in 2 tablespoons of butter until it is soft and browned. Add ½ cup of finely diced lean bacon, or ham with a little of its fat, and cook slowly until the bacon or ham is lightly browned. Then add a mixture, a generous ½ pound in all, of raw chicken livers and hearts, and the meat of cooked gizzards, all of these first very finely diced. Stir and cook the meat briefly. Now add 1 cup of dry white wine, and simmer until the liquid is reduced by two thirds. Add ¾ cup of Tomato Sauce (*see* Index), and salt and pepper to taste, and simmer the sauce to a good thick consistency. Serves six.

160

OLIVE ORCHARD   *Liguria*

Fritter Batter

Pastella

(Flour, olive oil, water, egg white)

Sift ¾ cup of flour, and stir into it 3 tablespoons of olive oil and ¾ cup of tepid water, or just enough to make a batter the consistency of smooth thin cream. Let it stand for 2 hours. When you are ready to use the batter, stir in 1 stiffly beaten egg white.

With this batter you may make banana or apple dessert fritters *(see* Index), or, with a little salt added to the batter, fritters of cooked vegetables, fish, shellfish, or meats, fried in deep hot oil. A "mixed fry," or *fritto misto,* is composed of small thin slices of veal or chicken breast, small pieces of brains and sweetbreads, and hearts of young artichokes, cauliflower flowerets, zucchini, and eggplant, or any combination of these that is obtainable.

HILLSIDE HOUSES AT MATERA   *Basilicata*

Fried Eggs Italian Style

Uova Fritte ali'Italiana

(Eggs, olive oil, Parmesan)

Heat ¼ cup of olive oil in a frying pan, break 4 eggs into it carefully, and fry them slowly over low heat in order not to toughen the whites. Remove the pan from the heat when the whites are almost set, and sprinkle each egg with a little salt and pepper and about ½ teaspoon of grated Parmesan. Put the pan in a 400° oven for 4 or 5 minutes, or until the cheese has melted. Serves four.

PASSO DI PORDOI   *Trentino-Alto Adige*

Sautéed Veal Kidneys
Rognoni Saltati

(Veal kidneys, butter, lemon, Marsala, Tomato Sauce)

Clean 3 medium veal kidneys of all fat and skin, open them partially to remove the white membranes at the core, and wash them well under running water. Slice them, dry the slices well, and flour them lightly. Heat 4 tablespoons of butter in a broad shallow pan and, when the butter is sizzling hot, add the kidneys and brown them quickly over moderately high heat. Add salt and pepper and the grated rind of ½ a lemon. Stir and turn the slices and do not overcook them; 4 minutes should suffice. Then add 3 tablespoons of Marsala or white wine, let it cook away almost entirely, and add 2 or 3 tablespoons of Tomato Sauce and a few drops of water, or just enough to keep the dish from being dry. Heat this quickly without letting it boil, sprinkle with finely chopped parsley, and serve at once. Serves four.

ISOLA BELLA ON LAKE MAGGIORE *Piedmont*

Veal Cutlet Hunter Style

Scaloppine di Vitello alla Cacciatora

(Veal, butter, oil, onion, garlic, mushrooms, tomatoes, orègano, parsley, wine)

Use a ½-inch-thick slice of veal from the leg weighing 1½ pounds. Season it with salt and pepper, and cook it for 5 minutes on each side in 3 tablespoons of hot butter. Do not let the butter brown. Cover the pan, lower the heat, and continue cooking the veal. In another pan, cook together 1 small chopped onion and 1 peeled and cut clove of garlic in 3 tablespoons of oil until the onion is soft and pale yellow. Add ¾ pound of small mushroom caps, or quartered caps if they are large, and cook for 6 to 8 minutes. Then remove the garlic, add 3 or 4 peeled, seeded, and coarsely chopped tomatoes (enough to make 2 cups), salt and pepper, ½ teaspoon of orègano, 1 teaspoon of minced parsley, and ⅓ cup of red wine. Simmer the sauce for 15 minutes or until it is of a good consistency. When the veal is tender, put it on a hot platter, pour the sauce over it, and serve. Serves four.

THE VILLAGE OF BRONZOLO   *Trentino-Alto Adige*

Mille Fanti Soup

Minestra Mille Fanti

(Stock, bread crumbs, Parmesan, nutmeg, eggs)

Have 5 cups of chicken stock (or Italian Broth) heating on the stove. Mix together ¾ cup of very finely crumbled fresh white bread, ⅜ cup of grated Parmesan cheese, salt, pepper, and a dash of nutmeg. Combine this mixture gradually with 3 beaten eggs, and blend well. When the soup is boiling, add the egg mixture to it a little at a time; you can either drop it in directly from a spoon, or force it through a colander into the soup, stirring well with a wire whisk after each addition. Cover the soup, let it simmer for 5 to 6 minutes, and stir well again before serving. Serve the soup at once, and pass Italian bread and more Parmesan with it. Serves six.

MANFREDONIA   *Puglie*

Fillets of Sole in Wine Sauce
Filetti di Pesce al Vino

(Sole or flounder, butter, raisins, lemon juice, white wine, Madeira or sherry)

Soak 2 or 3 tablespoons of white seedless raisins in water until they are softened. Dip 1½ pounds of sole or flounder fillets lightly in flour. Melt 4 tablespoons of butter in a skillet. When it is hot but not brown, add the fish, salt and pepper it, and add 2 teaspoons of lemon juice and the drained raisins. Cover the pan, and cook the fish slowly for 10 to 15 minutes, depending on the thickness of the fillets. Then turn each fillet with care, and add ¼ cup each of dry white wine and dry Madeira or sherry. Bring the liquid to a boil, then simmer gently for 2 or 3 minutes. Serves four.

ROMAN AQUEDUCT *Latium*

Chicory Roman Style

Cicorea alla Romana

(Curly chicory, olive oil, garlic, anchovies, tomatoes, chicken stock)

Wash 2 small heads of young and tender curly chicory, and shred it rather coarsely. Heat ¼ cup of olive oil in a saucepan with 2 cut cloves of garlic. When the garlic browns, discard it. Cut up 6 anchovy fillets, and stir them in the oil in the pan until they dissolve. Add 3 peeled and chopped tomatoes, the chicory, salt and pepper, and ¼ cup of chicken stock. Cover the pan closely, and cook the vegetables very slowly for about 30 minutes. The vegetables should be moist but not watery. Serves four.

167

TEMPLE OF SAN ANGELO—PERUGIA   *Umbria*

Vanilla Custard
Crema alla Vaniglia

(Eggs, sugar, milk, vanilla)

In the top of a double boiler beat together until well blended 3 eggs and 4 egg yolks. Stir in ½ cup of sugar, and add gradually, beating well all the time, 3½ cups of rich hot milk. Place the pan over hot but not boiling water, and cook the custard for about 8 minutes, stirring well. When it coats the spoon, remove it from the heat and let it cool. Stir in 1 teaspoon of vanilla. Makes about 4 cups. This custard has many uses in desserts, among them in the famous Italian *Zuppa Inglese* (*see* Index).

MONREALE HILLSIDE *Sicily*

Tomato Toast

Crostini di Pomidori

(Bread, onion, butter, tomatoes, egg yolk, cheese, Worcestershire sauce)

Over a low fire soften 1 small chopped onion in butter until it is pale gold. Add 3 peeled, seeded, and chopped tomatoes and salt and pepper. Cook together slowly until the liquid is evaporated and the mixture is thick. Cool it, and mix in 1 egg yolk, 2 tablespoons of grated cheese (Parmesan or Cheddar), and a few drops of Worcestershire sauce. Toast 4 slices of bread on one side; these may be left whole (with crusts removed), if the *crostini* are to be served as a first course, or first cut into 16 small squares if you wish to serve them as cocktail hors-d'oeuvre. Mound the tomato mixture on the untoasted side of the bread, and heat in a hot oven or under the broiler. Serve bubbling hot.

169

THE BAPTISTRY—FLORENCE   *Tuscany*

Sautéed Sweetbreads with Mushrooms
Scaloppine d'Animelle ai Funghi
(Sweetbreads, butter, mushrooms, onion, ham, Tomato Sauce)

Soak 2 pairs of sweetbreads in cold water for an hour. Drain them, cover them with cold salted water, bring this gradually to a boil, and poach the sweetbreads gently for about 10 minutes. Drain them again, plunge them into cold water, and let them cool in it. Remove the tough membranes, and cut the sweetbreads into rather thick slices. Dry the slices well, salt and flour them lightly, and brown them slowly in 4 tablespoons of hot butter for about 4 minutes on each side. They should have a lovely golden color and not be overcooked.

Meanwhile, wash, dry, and chop finely ¼ pound of mushrooms and chop 1 small onion. Cook these together in 3 tablespoons of butter until they are lightly browned. Add 2 tablespoons of finely chopped cooked ham, ¼ cup of Tomato Sauce, and salt and pepper. Cover the pan with greased paper or foil and a closely fitting lid, and cook the mixture over very low heat until it is quite thick. Arrange the sweetbreads on a hot platter, spoon some of the mushroom mixture onto each slice, and serve at once. Serves four.

170

PONTE VECCHIO—FLORENCE   *Tuscany*

Broccoli Florentine Style

Broccoli alla Fiorentina

(*Broccoli, garlic, olive oil*)

Wash 1½ pounds of broccoli. Divide the tops into flowerets; peel the stems and cut them into sections. In a saucepan, half cover the broccoli with boiling salted water, and cook it for about 10 minutes, or until it is done but still a little firm. Drain it well, and reserve some of the water. Put the broccoli in a saucepan with ¼ cup of its cooking water, 1 chopped clove of garlic, salt and pepper, and ⅓ cup of olive oil. Bring it quickly to a boil, then lower the heat and simmer the broccoli briefly. Serves four.

171

THE PORT—SAN REMO *Liguria*

Broiled Scallops
Conchigli ai Ferri

(Scallops, bacon, olive oil, butter, scallion, garlic, parsley)

Thread fresh scallops and squares of not too thinly sliced bacon alternately on small skewers; allow about 1 pound of scallops to serve four. Broil the filled skewers under a hot flame, turning them to cook on all sides. Serve with the following sauce: In a small saucepan heat together 3 tablespoons of good olive oil, 1½ tablespoons of butter, 1 finely minced scallion, 1 peeled and cut clove of garlic, and 1 tablespoon of minced parsley, and season with salt and pepper. Heat the mixture and let it steep, covered, without boiling or browning, for about 5 minutes. Remove the pieces of garlic, and pour the sauce over the skewered scallops. Serves four.

FARM NEAR POGGIO DI BRETTA   *Marche*

Rice with Eggs
Minestra Bordolese
(Stock, rice, eggs, lemon, Parmesan)

Heat 1½ cups of chicken stock (or Italian Broth), and when it is boiling add ½ cup of rice. Cover, and cook over low heat until the rice is tender and the broth is absorbed. Beat 4 eggs thoroughly together with the juice of a small lemon. Off the fire, add this to the rice and stir the mixture well until it has a creamy consistency. Then stir in 3 tablespoons of grated Parmesan. This serves two if eaten by itself as a *minestra,* which in Italian-style dining means a hot dish, not necessarily a soup, that precedes the main course. It serves four as an accompaniment to, for instance, roast or broiled chicken.

THE FORUM   *Rome*

Cold Poached Partridge
Pernici in Brodo
(Partridge, onion, celery, herbs, tomato sauce, oil, vinegar)

Put 3 drawn partridge in a large saucepan with water almost to cover, and add salt, 1 small onion, a few celery leaves, a few leaves of basil, a sprig of parsley, and 3 tablespoons of tomato sauce. Cover, and simmer the partridge very slowly until they are tender but still whole and firm. Drain them from the broth, carve them into halves or quarters, and sprinkle them with olive oil, wine vinegar, minced parsley, and salt and pepper. Let them marinate until they are cold, and serve them with a green salad. This is a particularly good way to prepare partridge that are no longer very young and tender. Serves six. The broth will make delicious soup.

PONTE FABRICIO   *Rome*

Cold Veal with Tuna Fish Sauce
Vitello Tonnato

(Veal, vegetables, wine, herbs, anchovies, tuna fish, olive oil, lemon juice, capers)

Tie a 2-pound piece of leg of tender young veal, free of all bone, gristle, and fat, neatly in a block. Soak it in cold water for 3 hours, changing the water several times. Drain and dry the meat, and place it in a heavy enamelled casserole just large enough to hold it comfortably. Add 1 onion stuck with 2 cloves, 1 small carrot and 1 small stalk of celery, both sliced, 1 bay leaf, salt, pepper, ½ cup of olive oil, and 1 cup each of white wine and water. Bring the liquid to a boil, cover the casserole, and simmer the veal for about 2 hours, or until it is tender. Let it cool in the liquid, then drain and dry the meat, and slice it thinly. Reassemble the slices in a block in a closely fitting deep earthenware dish or *terrine*.

Cut up 4 or 5 anchovy fillets, and work them in a mortar with a 3½-ounce can of tuna fish, discarding most of the oil in the can. When the mixture is smooth, add very gradually about ½ cup of olive oil, stirring well with a fork as in making mayonnaise. Add gradually the juice of 1 large lemon and 2 or 3 tablespoons of dry white wine. The sauce should have the consistency of cream or a rather thin mayonnaise. Add pepper and 2 tablespoons of washed and dried salted Italian capers. Cover the veal completely with the sauce and decorate with slices of peeled lemon and sour pickles. Serve cold. Serves eight.

175

THE MATTRESS MAKER—CIVIDALE DEL FRIULI   *Friuli-Venezia Giulia*

Ravioli with Ricotta Filling
Ravioli di Ricotta
(Homemade Pasta, butter, egg, Ricotta, Parmesan, seasonings, parsley)

Roll out two thin sheets of Homemade *Pasta*. On one sheet place teaspoonfuls of Ricotta filling (*see* below) in even rows, 1½ inches apart. Place the second sheet loosely over the first, and press the two layers of *pasta* together gently between the mounds of filling. With a little wooden wheel cutter, cut the *ravioli* into squares, and check that the edges are well sealed together. Place the *ravioli* gently in boiling salted water, and cook them for about 5 minutes, or until they rise to the surface. Remove them with a slotted spoon as they are done and place them in a heated serving dish. Dress them with melted butter and grated Parmesan, or with Tomato Sauce (*see* Index) and Parmesan. Serves six.

Ricotta filling: Cream 2 tablespoons of butter and mix in thoroughly 1 egg yolk. Add ¾ pound of Ricotta cheese and ¾ cup of grated Parmesan, and work the mixture until it is smooth. Stir in 2 tablespoons of finely chopped parsley, salt and pepper, and a dash of nutmeg.

ASSISI   *Umbria*

Eggs in Snow
Uova nella Neve

(Mashed potatoes, Mozzarella cheese, eggs, butter, Parmesan)

Peel and boil 1 pound of potatoes; drain and mash them, and beat into them a good lump of butter, salt, and ½ to 1 cup of milk, or enough to make a creamy, smooth purée. Spread the purée in a shallow buttered baking dish, and cover it with a single layer of thinly sliced Mozzarella cheese (about 3½ ounces). Into this, with the back of a big spoon, press 6 shallow hollows, and break an egg into each hollow. Sprinkle the egg with salt, pepper, and grated Parmesan, and dot them generously with butter. Bake the dish in a 400° oven until the eggs are set and the cheese is melted. Serves six.

THE MATTERHORN   *Valle d'Aosta*

Pea Soup Peasant Style
Zuppa di Piselli alla Paesana
(Peas, onion, butter, bacon, tomatoes, chicken stock, bread, Parmesan)

Peel and chop 1 onion and put it in a saucepan with 3 tablespoons of butter and ¼ pound of diced bacon. Cook the mixture over moderate heat until the onion is lightly browned. Peel, seed, and chop 2 tomatoes, and shell 3 pounds of peas. Add the vegetables to the saucepan, season with just a little salt and pepper, and let the vegetables cook, stirring occasionally, for 2 or 3 minutes. Add gradually about 4½ cups of chicken stock or Italian Broth. The soup should be of a rather thick consistency. Simmer it until the peas are well cooked. Serve the soup poured over thin toasted slices of Italian or French bread covered with grated Parmesan. Serves six.

OLGIASCA, ON LAKE COMO   *Lombardy*

Shin of Veal Milanese
Osso Buco Milanese

(Veal shin, carrot, celery, onion, tomato paste, wine, stock, lemon, parsley, garlic)

Have the butcher saw the meaty part of shin of young veal (foreleg) into four slices 2 or more inches thick. In a heavy pot, brown these well on all sides in 2 tablespoons each of hot butter and olive oil. Season them with salt and pepper, and add ½ a carrot, grated, and 1 small celery stalk and 1 medium onion, both chopped. Cook the mixture for about 8 minutes, or until the vegetables are softened. Then blend in 2 teaspoons of flour, stir in 2 tablespoons of tomato paste, and add 1 cup of dry white wine and enough hot stock or water to come just to the top of the meat. The veal should be placed in one layer, each slice standing upright so the bones and marrow will stay in the meat. Cover the casserole and simmer the veal very slowly for about 2 hours, or until it is very tender, adding a little hot liquid if necessary. Remove the meat, strain the sauce, and remove any fat that rises to the surface. Replace the meat in the casserole, add the sauce and a mixture, called *gremolada,* consisting of the grated rind of half a lemon, 1 tablespoon of finely minced parsley, and 1 minced clove of garlic. Reheat and simmer all together for 2 minutes. Serve with boiled rice or *Risotto.* Serves four.

RAGUSA   *Sicily*

Potato Sticks

Bastoncini di Patate

(Potatoes, flour, butter, Parmesan, egg)

Boil in their skins enough potatoes to make ¾ cup when they are peeled and mashed. Beat the mashed potatoes well, and measure out the ¾ cupful. Add 1 cup of flour, 6 tablespoons of softened butter, ¾ cup of grated Parmesan cheese, and a little salt. Work the mixture together like a dough, and spread it out on a board in a layer less than ½ inch thick. Cut it into sticks the size of your little finger and place these in a buttered baking sheet. Brush them with beaten egg and bake them in a 400° oven for about 20 minutes. Serve as a hot hors-d'oeuvre.

CAPRI   *Campania*

Aparagus Tips with Prosciutto
Asparagi con Prosciutto
(Asparagus, prosciutto or ham, butter, Parmesan)

Cook 2 dozen asparagus tips in boiling salted water for 10 to 15 minutes, or until they are tender, and drain them well. Wrap the asparagus in bundles of three in thin slices of *prosciutto* or cooked ham, pinning each little package with a wooden toothpick. Butter a shallow baking dish, place the packages in it in one layer, and sprinkle them with grated Parmesan and melted butter. Bake them in a 400° oven for 5 minutes, or until the cheese has melted. Add a little more melted butter before serving. Serves four.

LAKE ORTA   *Piedmont*

Peas with Fennel

Piselli al Finocchio

(Peas, fennel, butter, nutmeg)

Shell 2½ pounds of fresh peas, and boil them in salted water with 1 small head of fennel until they are tender. Drain the vegetables, and chop the fennel and rub it through a sieve. In a wide saucepan, melt 2½ tablespoons of butter, and add the peas, salt and pepper, and a dash of nutmeg. Stir well together for a few seconds, add the fennel purée, reheat, and serve in a hot dish. Serves four.

CITY FOUNTAIN—VITERBO   *Latium*

Apricot Omelette
Frittata Dolce con la Marmellata

(Eggs, salt, lemon rind, butter, apricot jam, sugar, rum)

Beat together 6 eggs and 3 teaspoons of water with a fork for half a minute until they are well blended. Add a small pinch of salt and the grated rind of half a lemon. Melt 2 tablespoons of butter in a hot omelette pan and, when the foam subsides, pour in the eggs. When the omelette is set and lightly browned on the bottom, turn it out flat onto a plate. Add a little butter to the pan if necessary, then slide the omelette back into the pan, and cook the other side lightly; do not overcook it. Turn the omelette out onto a board, spread 3 or 4 tablespoons of apricot jam over it, roll it up, and place it on an oval heatproof platter. Sprinkle the surface evenly with fine granulated sugar. Pour ¼ cup of warmed rum over the omelette, set it aflame, and serve immediately. Or, if you have an iron poker you can heat to the scorching point, caramelize the sugar on the omelette in crisscross diagonal lines with the poker, and omit the blazing rum. Serves four.

FEBRUARY AT AGRIGENTO *Sicily*

Buttered Carrots

Carote al Burro

(Carrots, butter, flour, chicken stock, cinnamon, lemon juice)

Wash and scrape half a dozen medium carrots, drop them into boiling salted water, and boil them for about 10 minutes. Drain them, cool them a little, and cut them in two across and then lengthwise into thin strips. Melt 3 tablespoons of butter in a broad saucepan, add the carrots and salt and pepper, and cook them over low heat, stirring often, until they are tender. Then sprinkle the carrots with ½ teaspoon of flour, blend it into the butter, and add ¼ cup of hot liquid composed of half chicken stock and half water. Simmer the mixture briefly, and add a tiny pinch of powdered cinnamon and a few drops of lemon juice. Serves four.

MARKET IN VENICE   *Veneto*

Salt Codfish Vicenza
Baccala Vicentina

(Salt codfish, butter, olive oil, onions, garlic, milk)

Soak 2 pounds of salt codfish fillets for 6 to 8 hours, changing the water several times. Heat 2 tablespoons of butter and ½ cup of olive oil in a broad shallow pan, add 2 finely sliced onions, and cook them slowly until they are soft but not browned. Add 2 cloves of garlic, chopped, the drained and dried codfish, and a little freshly ground pepper. Cook the fish slowly for 5 to 10 minutes. Then place the pan on an asbestos mat, add enough hot milk to cover the fish, and cover the pan. Simmer the fish very gently for about 1 hour, or until it is tender and the sauce is reduced and slightly thickened. Serve with boiled potatoes. Serves six.

WINTER DAY AT MINORI   *Campania*

Potato and Egg Salad
Insalata di Patate e Uova

(Potatoes, eggs, onion, celery, parsley, anchovies, vinegar, oil)

Boil 4 large potatoes until they are done but still firm. Cool, peel, and dice them. Hard-boil 4 eggs, and peel and quarter them. Place the potatoes in a layer in a salad bowl and arrange the eggs over them. Sprinkle the salad with 1 table-spoon of chopped mild Italian onion, ½ cup of chopped celery, and 2 teaspoons of finely minced parsley. Over all pour the following dressing: Cut up and mash 3 anchovy fillets, add freshly ground pepper, and stir in 2 tablespoons of wine vinegar and 6 tablespoons of olive oil. Add salt if needed. Chill the salad in the refrigerator before serving. This makes an excellent first-course hors-d'oeuvre. Serves six.

THE CATHEDRAL—SPOLETO   *Umbria*

Tomato Salad with Basil

Insalata di Pomidori con Basilico

(Tomatoes, fresh basil, wine vinegar, olive oil, garlic)

Slice or quarter 4 firm ripe tomatoes and arrange them on a serving dish. Sprinkle over them 1½ tablespoons of fresh chopped basil leaves. Spoon over the salad a dressing made of ½ tablespoon of wine vinegar, 4 tablespoons of olive oil, ½ clove of garlic, chopped and mashed, and salt and pepper to taste. Serve as a first-course hors-d'oeuvre or *antipasto*. Serves four.

187

SUMMER LANDSCAPE   *Tuscany*

Meat Loaf Florentine

Polpettone alla Fiorentina

(Veal or beef, ham, spices, egg, flour, oil, butter, vegetables, lemon)

Put through a meat grinder 1 pound of lean veal or beef together with a ¼ -pound piece of ham, including some fat. Mix into the meat salt, pepper, a pinch each of nutmeg and cinnamon, and finally 1 egg. Form the mixture into one flattened ball and roll it in flour. In a heavy saucepan heat together 3 tablespoons of olive oil and 2 tablespoons of butter. In this brown slowly 1 small onion, ½ stalk of celery, and 1 small carrot, all very finely minced, and 1 teaspoon of chopped parsley. When the vegetables take on a little color, put in the meat ball and brown it slowly on both sides. Blend ½ tablespoon of flour into ½ cup of water, and add this and a little more salt to the pan. Cover, and simmer the meat for ½ an hour, or until it is cooked through. Turn it occasionally, see that it does not stick to the pan, and add a little hot water if necessary. Place the meat loaf on a hot platter and squeeze the juice of half a lemon over it. Force the pan juices and vegetables through a sieve (or purée them in an electric blender), and pour this sauce over the meat. Serves four.

CASTLE NEAR SANTA CRISTINA   *Trentino-Alto Adige*

Mushrooms on Toast

Crostini di Funghi

(Mushrooms, butter, lemon juice, flour, chicken broth, wine, egg yolk, croutons)

Clean and slice ¾ pound of mushrooms. In a skillet cook them in 3 tablespoons of hot butter, together with a little lemon juice, for about 5 minutes. Make a sauce by blending ¾ tablespoon of flour into 1 tablespoon of melted butter and stirring in gradually ½ cup of chicken broth and ¼ cup of white wine. Keep the heat low. Add salt and pepper if needed. Simmer the sauce, stirring, until it is slightly thickened. Removed it from the heat and quickly stir in 1 egg yolk. Add the mushrooms and spoon the mixture onto triangles of bread fried in butter. Serves two.

189

PIAZZA DEL DUOMO—LECCE   *Puglie*

Bread Sticks

Grissini

(Flour, yeast, water, salt, sugar, butter, milk)

Dissolve 1 teaspoon of dry yeast in ⅓ cup of tepid water. Combine this with 1 cup of sifted flour, knead the mixture for 5 minutes, and leave it in a floured bowl, covered with a damp cloth, for 2 hours. Sift together 1 cup of flour, 1 teaspoon of salt, and 1 teaspoon of sugar. Add to this 3 tablespoons of melted butter and ¼ cup of tepid milk. Mix these ingredients into a dough, add it to the first "sponge," and knead the two together for 6 to 7 minutes. Let this dough stand again in the floured bowl for about 2 hours, or until double in bulk. Knead it again for a few minutes, then divide it into 3 equal sections and divide each section into 12 parts, more or less, to make about 3 dozen *grissini*. Roll each bit of dough, on the bread board and between the palms of your hands, into a long thin roll. Place them, at least an inch apart, on greased baking sheets, and press the end with your thumbs to anchor them lightly to the baking sheets. Brush them with milk and bake them in a 400° oven for 12 minutes, or until they are golden brown. Let them cool, and store them in a tin box with a tight cover.

PIAZZA DELLA COMMENDA—GENOA   *Liguria*

Noodles with Pesto

Trenette col Pesto

(Noodles, butter, Parmesan, garlic, fresh basil, pine nuts, olive oil)

Noodles in Genoa are called *trenette* and are cut in long strips the shape and width of a match stick. Boil 1 pound of Homemade *Pasta* cut in this way for 5 minutes in salted water. Drain them, and add at once the following sauce and a generous spoonful of soft butter which are mixed into the noodles at table. Pass grated Parmesan separately. Serves six.

Pesto: Chop finely 5 to 6 cloves of garlic. Remove the stems from a bunch of fresh basil. Most Italian recipes call for "a good handful," as this is an ingredient it seems impossible to measure accurately; about 2 cups of leaves will do. Chop the leaves with a little salt, as this helps keep them green; a little parsley added to the basil also contributes color to this sauce which should be a fresh green. Work the garlic and leaves to a paste in a mortar, and add 2 tablespoons of pine nuts and ⅓ cup of grated Parmesan or Pecorino cheese. Continue working the mixture to a very smooth paste, then add gradually ¼ cup of olive oil, stirring well, until the mixture has the consistency of creamed butter or mayonnaise. All this may also be done in an electric blender. *Pesto* may be served with any type of hot *pasta,* and a spoonful added to Italian soups such as Minestrone is delicious.

191

CHURCH OF SANTA CROCE—FLORENCE *Tuscany*

Apricot Soufflé Pudding
Budino di Albicocche

(Apricots, sugar, lemon rind, sweet butter, eggs)

Cook an 11-ounce package of dried apricots according to the directions on the package, using 3 tablespoons of sugar. Mash and strain (or purée in an electric blender) enough of them to make ½ cup. To this add ½ cup of fine granulated sugar and the grated rind of ½ a lemon; work these together well. Soften ¼ pound of fresh sweet butter and cream it well. Work 5 egg yolks into the butter, one at a time, adding also ¼ teaspoon of salt. Combine the two mixtures, and continue stirring long and thoroughly. Then fold in 5 stiffly beaten egg whites. Pour the mixture into a deep, buttered 1½-quart baking dish or soufflé mold. Place the mold in a pan of boiling water, and bake it in a 350° oven for 35 minutes. This is an exquisite soufflé, soft and creamy in the center. It should be served at once, hot from the dish. Serves four.

HILLSIDE CHURCH—MONSELICE   *Veneto Euganea*

Chicken Orègano
Pollo Oreganato

(Chicken, lemon juice, olive oil, garlic, parsley, orègano)

Cut a 3½-pound broiler into four pieces, and salt and pepper them. Dip each piece into a mixture composed of ¼ cup of lemon juice, ⅓ cup of olive oil, 1 minced clove of garlic, 1 teaspoon of chopped parsley, and 2 teaspoons of orègano. Cook them under the broiler for 15 to 20 minutes on each side, or until they are brown and tender, basting occasionally with more of the oil, lemon, and herb mixture. Serve with the pan juices poured over the chicken. Serves four.

TORBOLE, ON LAKE GARDA   *Trentino-Alto Adige*

Aparagus Soup
Zuppa di Asparagi

(Asparagus, potatoes, leek, butter, cream, egg yolk, croutons)

Clean and scrape 2 pounds of asparagus; peel 2 potatoes and cut them into small pieces; wash 1 leek well and slice the white part thin. Put these vegetables in a saucepan, add 5½ cups of water, or enough to cover them well, and boil them, uncovered, until tender. Cut the tips from the asparagus and reserve them. Force the rest of the vegetables, with the liquid, through a strainer. Return the soup to the saucepan and add 2 tablespoons of butter, salt to taste, and the asparagus tips. Beat together in a tureen 1 egg yolk and ½ cup of cream. Reheat the soup just until it boils, and pour it into the tureen, stirring well. Serve with bread croutons fried in butter. Serves six.

194

BERGAMO   *Lombardy*

Fontina Cheese Mold
Sformato di Fontina

(Fontina cheese, butter, flour, milk, eggs, tomato sauce)

Slice thinly ½ pound of Fontina cheese and soak the slices for an hour or more in cold water. Make a thick cream sauce by blending 4 tablespoons of flour into 3 tablespoons of melted butter and adding gradually 1 cup of milk. Add salt and pepper, and cook the sauce, stirring until it has thickened. Add the drained slices of cheese, a few at a time, and stir until they have melted. Allow the mixture to cool a little, then add 4 beaten egg yolks, and fold in the stiffly beaten whites. Butter a soufflé mold and dust it lightly with fine bread crumbs. Pour in the cheese mixture to fill the mold by two thirds, and cover it with a piece of buttered paper. Stand the mold in a pan of hot water, place it in a 400° oven, and cook it for 10 minutes. Then reduce the heat to 325° and cook the mold for about 40 minutes more. Turn it out onto a hot platter, and serve it with a delicate tomato sauce made of fresh tomatoes. Serves six.

MOUNTAIN FARMHOUSES AT MAEN *Valle d'Aosta*

Chicken Mountaineer
Pollo alla Montagnuola
(Chicken, eggs, butter, bread crumbs, parsley, lemon)

Cut a 3½-pound chicken into eight serving pieces, and salt and pepper them. Dip them into 2 eggs first beaten together with 2 tablespoons of water. Coat the chicken completely and let it stand in the beaten egg for an hour. Melt 2 tablespoons of butter in a casserole, tipping it to coat the inside well. Roll the pieces of chicken in fine bread crumbs and put them in the casserole. Cover, and bake in a 350° oven for 1½ hours in all. Twenty minutes before the chicken is done, baste it with a little melted butter and finish the cooking uncovered; the chicken should brown, and if it doesn't do so properly in the oven, put the pieces briefly on a rack under a hot broiler. Serve on a hot platter, sprinkled with minced parsley and surrounded with wedges of lemon. Serves four.

STORM OVER GENOA   *Liguria*

Cold Duck Genoa Style
Anitre Fredde alla Genovese

(Ducks, herbs, shallots, anchovies, mustard, eggs, capers, pickles, vinegar, oil)

Roast 2 ducks and put them aside to cool. Remove the fat from the roasting pan and reserve the remaining brown juices. Make a remoulade sauce: In a mortar combine 2 teaspoons of parsley, 1 teaspoon each of chervil and tarragon, and 2 shallots, all finely chopped, and 3 anchovy fillets, 1 teaspoon of French mixed mustard, the yolks of 4 hard-boiled eggs, 1 teaspoon of salted capers (first rinsed and dried), 3 small sour gherkins, finely chopped, pepper, and a little salt. Work all together thoroughly with a pestle. Then mix in 1 raw egg yolk, 2 tablespoons of wine vinegar, ½ cup of olive oil, and some of the reserved brown juices from the duck. Beat this sauce thoroughly.

Carve the ducks and arrange the pieces on a platter; the handsomest way is to reassemble them on the carcasses in the forms of whole ducks. The platter may be decorated with black olives, cooked shrimp, and slices of lemon. Pass the sauce separately. Serves eight.

.TAORMINA   *Sicily*

Tea Cookies

I Bicciolani

(Butter, sugar, cinnamon, lemon rind, cocoa, flour, cornstarch, eggs)

Cream together ⅞ cup of butter (two ¼-pound sticks less 2 tablespoons) and 4 tablespoons of sugar. Add a good pinch of cinnamon, the finely grated rind of 1 small lemon, and 1 tablespoon of cocoa or powdered chocolate. Mix thoroughly, and add gradually 1¾ cups of sifted flour, ⅜ cup of cornstarch, 1 whole egg, and 2 egg yolks. Beat this to a smooth paste, and let it rest overnight in the refrigerator. Then roll it out on a floured board into a layer about ½ inch or less thick. Cut the dough into rectangles about 1 inch wide and 1½ inches long. Place the cookies on greased baking sheets, and bake them in a 375° oven for 10 to 15 minutes, or until they are firm and lightly browned. Cool them on wire cake racks, and store in a tin box with a tight cover.

198

CANAL NEAR PISA   *Tuscany*

Turnips with Béchamel Sauce
Rape alla Besciamella

(White turnips, butter, onion, flour, milk, Parmesan)

Peel 2 pounds of young white turnips and slice them very thin. Heat 4 table-spoons of butter in a broad pan, add the turnips, turn and stir them in the butter, and add about ¼ cup of water. Cook the turnips very slowly, until they are done but still a little firm and all the water has evaporated. Do not let them brown. Season them with salt and pepper.

In another saucepan, melt 2 tablespoons of butter, add a slice of onion, and cook it slowly until it is golden. Discard the onion. Blend 2 tablespoons of flour into the butter, gradually add 2 cups of milk, add salt and pepper, and simmer the sauce, stirring, for 2 or 3 minutes. Add ⅓ cup of grated Parmesan, mix well, and pour the sauce over the turnips. Serves six.

PIAZZA DEL POPOLO—ASCOLI PICENO *Marche*

Hot Cheese Balls
Polpettine di Formaggio

(Bread crumbs, Parmesan, nutmeg, parsley, eggs, flour, olive oil)

Mix together 1½ cups of crumbled fresh bread crumbs, 2 cups of grated Parmesan, salt and pepper, a good dash of nutmeg, and 2 teaspoons of finely minced parsley, and stir in 3 lightly beaten eggs. Form the mixture into little balls about the size of walnuts, roll them in flour, and dip them in egg beaten with a few drops of water. Drop the cheese balls into deep hot olive oil, and fry them until they are golden. Serves four as a first course or as a luncheon dish with a salad.

THE FORUM—POMPEII   *Campania*

Peas with Mushrooms
Piselli ai Funghi

(Peas, mushrooms, carrot, herbs, lettuce, sugar, butter)

Shell 2 pounds of tender young peas; clean and slice ½ pound of mushrooms; scrape and slice 1 small carrot; and tie together a bouquet consisting of a sprig of celery leaves, a sprig of parsley, a sprig of fresh thyme, and half a bay leaf. Shred coarsely the heart of a head of tender garden lettuce, put it in a heavy saucepan, add the peas, the other vegetables and the bouquet, salt and pepper, 1 teaspoon of sugar, ¼ cup of water, and 2 tablespoons of butter. Cover the pan closely and put it on an asbestos mat over low heat. Cook the peas slowly for about 45 minutes, more or less, until they are tender and the liquid is almost entirely evaporated. Stir them from time to time. Remove the bouquet before serving. Serves four.

OUTDOOR PULPIT—CATHEDRAL AT PRATO *Tuscany*

Asparagus Sunday Style
Asparagi alla Domenicana

(Asparagus, eggs, anchovies, olive oil, mustard, parsley, vinegar, lemon)

Clean and peel 2 pounds of asparagus, cutting off the tough ends. Tie it in a bunch, and cook it in boiling salted water for 20 minutes, or until it is tender but not overcooked. Drain the asparagus, arrange it on an oval platter, and serve it warm with the following cold sauce: Sieve the yolks of 3 hard-boiled eggs and 2 anchovy fillets. Add 2 raw egg yolks, mix well, and add, drop by drop, stirring constantly, 1 cup of olive oil, as in making mayonnaise. Add salt, pepper, 1 teaspoon of mild mixed mustard, 1 teaspoon of finely minced parsley, 1 teaspoon of wine vinegar, and the juice of half a lemon, or more to taste. Serves four to six.

SAN FRUTTUOSO   *Liguria*

Roast Duck Genoa
Anitra Arrosto alla Genovese

(Duck, olive oil, parsley, bay leaf, stock, lemon juice)

Put a duck in a deep oval dish, salt and pepper it well, add a teaspoon of chopped parsley and a crumbled bay leaf, and pour over it ½ cup of olive oil. Let the duck stand for 4 to 5 hours in this marinade, and turn it from time to time. Preheat the oven to 450°. Drain the duck from the marinade, put it in a roasting pan, and when you put the duck in the oven, lower the heat to 350°. Roast the duck until it is done, allowing 20 minutes to the pound; prick the skin well in the fattest places to release the fat. When the duck is three quarters cooked, remove most of the fat from the pan, and stir ¼ cup of stock and the juice of 1 lemon into the pan juices. Baste the duck with these juices several times, and serve them as a sauce for the duck. Serves four.

AZZENZA   *Veneto*

Banana Fritters

Fritelle di Banane

(Bananas, sugar, lemon juice, brandy, Fritter Batter, oil)

Cut 4 ripe bananas in half lengthwise, then cut the pieces in half crosswise.
Sprinkle them with 3 tablespoons of sugar, about 3 teaspoons of lemon juice, and
4 tablespoons of brandy. Let the bananas marinate for 2 hours, then drain them,
and dip them in Fritter Batter *(see* Index). In a skillet, fry them in deep hot oil
until they are golden. Sprinkle the fritters with sugar and serve at once. Serves
four. Apple slices may be used in the same way.

MUGGIA   *Friuli-Venezia Giulia*

Lobster Fra Diavolo

Aragosta Fra Diavolo

(Lobsters, olive oil, garlic, tomato purée, red wine, herbs, red pepper flakes)

Heat ¼ cup of olive oil in a saucepan, add 2 finely chopped cloves of garlic, and cook them slowly for 1 minute. Add 2 cups of tomato purée, ½ cup of red wine, 1 tablespoon of chopped parsley, 1 teaspoon of orégano, a pinch of dried red pepper flakes, and salt to taste. Simmer the sauce slowly for about 20 minutes, stirring occasionally, until it is somewhat reduced and thickened. Meanwhile, boil four 1¼-pound lobsters for 12 minutes. Drain and split them, and crack the large claws. Lay the lobsters in a large baking dish, split sides up, spoon the sauce over them, and bake them for about 7 minutes in a preheated 350° oven. Serves four.

205

THE PIAZZA BATTISTI—TRENTO   *Trentino-Alto Adige*

Chicken Mold

Sformato di Pollo

(Chicken, butter, flour, milk, nutmeg, egg, Hollandaise sauce)

Remove the meat from half of a 5½-pound boiled fowl. Put the clear meat through a grinder and reserve it. Make a thick white sauce by blending 6 tablespoons of flour into 4 tablespoons of melted butter and adding gradually 2¼ cups of milk. Season the sauce well with salt and pepper and a good dash of nutmeg. When it is perfectly smooth and thickened, let it cool somewhat, then stir in 3 egg yolks. Beat the whites stiff, fold them into the mixture, then fold in the chicken meat. Butter a soufflé mold or a tube cake mold, coat it lightly with fine bread crumbs, and pour in the chicken mixture to fill the dish by about two thirds. Cover it with a buttered paper, stand it in a pan of hot water, and cook it in a 325° oven for about 1 hour, or until a thin skewer or a knife inserted in the center of the dish comes out clean. Turn the mold out onto a hot platter, and serve it with Hollandaise sauce. Serves six.

PORTOFINO   *Liguria*

Shellfish Soup
Zuppa di Crostacei

(Clams, lobster, crabs, olive oil, onion, garlic, herbs, tomatoes, wine, saffron)

All the shellfish that go into this soup are, of course, fresh and uncooked. Scrub the shells of 3 dozen small clams; cut a live 1½-pound lobster into 4 to 6 pieces; and remove the legs from 6 or 8 crabs, discarding the bodies. Your fish dealer can do all of this for you. In an earthen casserole heat ⅓ cup of olive oil, and add 2 chopped onions, 4 minced cloves of garlic, 1 tablespoon of chopped parsley, and 2 peeled, seeded, and coarsely chopped tomatoes. Cook all together for 5 or 6 minutes over moderate heat, then add ¾ cup of dry white wine. Let this simmer and reduce a little for 5 more minutes. Now add the shellfish, 1½ to 2 cups of boiling water, a bay leaf, a good pinch of saffron, and salt and pepper. Cook the soup over a rather brisk fire for 15 minutes. At the last, melt in 1 tablespoon of butter, moving the casserole with a rotary motion to swirl it in. Pour the broth into hot soup plates, over slices of French or Italian bread which have been fried crisp in butter. Serve the shellfish at the same time from a separate heated bowl. Serves four.

PERUGIA   *Umbria*

Eggs Poached in Tomato Sauce
Uova Affogate in Pomodoro

(Eggs, olive oil, onion, tomatoes, parsley, red pepper flakes)

Heat ¼ cup of olive oil in a large skillet, add 1 finely minced onion, and cook it slowly until it is transparent and pale gold in color. Add 2½ cups (20 ounces) of canned Italian tomatoes (or the equivalent in peeled and chopped fresh tomatoes), 1 tablespoon of finely chopped parsley, a pinch of dried red pepper flakes, and salt to taste. Simmer the sauce, covered, over low heat for 20 to 30 minutes, or until the flavors are well amalgamated. Or, you may heat a can of good tomato sauce, adding the desired seasonings. One at a time. break 6 eggs into the sauce, spacing them evenly. Cook them very slowly, covered, until the whites are set. Serves six.

BOLOGNA   *Emilia-Romagna*

Sausages in Tomato Sauce Romagna

Salsiccie con Pomodoro alla Romagnola

(Italian sausages, oil, sage, tomatoes or Tomato Sauce)

Prick the skins of 1 pound of fresh, Italian sweet pork sausages. Heat 1 or 2 tablespoons of olive oil in a heavy skillet, and add the sausages, whole or cut in sections, as you prefer, and 2 or 3 leaves of sage or a good pinch of dried sage. Cook them slowly until they have browned a little on all sides; if the sausages have given off a large quantity of fat, remove some of it at this point. Then add 2 peeled, seeded, and coarsely chopped tomatoes, or 1 cup of Tomato Sauce *(see* Index), and cook the mixture slowly for 15 minutes. Serves four.

FONTANEZZO IN THE DOLOMITES *Trentino-Alto Adige*

Chick Peas with Fennel
Ceci con Finocchio

(Chick peas, olive oil, garlic, red pepper, fennel, Tomato Sauce, onion, salt pork)

Wash 2 cups of dried chick peas, cover them with cold water, and soak them overnight. Put the chick peas and their water in a large saucepan, add enough water to cover by about 2 inches, add salt, and simmer them for 2 hours, or until they are tender. Drain the peas and reserve the cooking water. In a shallow pan heat 3 tablespoons of olive oil, and add 1 minced clove of garlic, ⅓ teaspoon of dried thyme, a pinch of dried red pepper flakes, and 2 cups of chopped fennel, green leafy tops and stems combined. Stir and cook this mixture slowly for 5 minutes. Add 1 cup of the cooking liquid from the chick peas.

Put the chick peas in a casserole, and add the fennel mixture, ½ cup of Tomato Sauce *(see* Index), 1 small sliced onion, and enough of the reserved cooking water almost to cover the peas. Mix well together and add salt if needed. Bury a 1½-inch square of salt pork in the center of the dish. Cover the casserole, and cook the chick peas in a 300° oven for 2 hours or more. Remove the cover for the last half hour of cooking. The completed dish should be quite moist. Serves six.

CHIOGGIA   *Veneto*

Fillets of Haddock Orègano
Filetti di Pesce Oreganato

(Haddock, olive oil, lemon, bread crumbs, garlic, parsley, orègano, raisins, butter)

Coat a shallow baking dish with olive oil, and arrange in it 2 pounds of fillets of haddock or other white fish suitable for baking, first salted lightly and brushed with oil. Sprinkle a little lemon juice over the fish. Combine ¾ cup of dry bread crumbs, 2 finely chopped cloves of garlic, a little salt, 1 teaspoon of finely minced parsley, and 1½ teaspoons of dried orègano. Spread this mixture over the fish, and add about ½ cup of hot water to the dish, spooning it over the bread-crumb coating. Bake the fish in a 400° oven for about 20 minutes in all. When it is half done, add 2 tablespoons of white raisins which have first been soaked in water to soften them, place a few slices of peeled lemon on the fish, and dot it with butter. The fish is cooked when it flakes easily with a fork. Serves six.

211

THE LAGOON AT GRADO   *Friuli-Venezia Giulia*

Grilled Grey Mullet

Cefali in Gratella

(Mullet or other small fish, olive oil, lemon)

The original recipe calls for two grey mullet, each weighing about 1¼ pounds. Of course you may substitute any comparable salt-water fish, including small bass, catfish, perch, and also mackerel. Wash and dry the cleaned fish, and place them in a shallow dish. Pour over them about 4 tablespoons of good olive oil and the juice of 1 lemon, and season them with salt and pepper. Let the fish marinate for about an hour. Heat the broiler grill well under a hot flame, and grease it with oil; have a broiler pan under it to catch the basting juices. Put the fish on the grill and cook them fairly close to the fire (about 3 inches away), basting them from time to time with the marinade. Turn them within 3 to 5 minutes, depending on the size of the fish, and cook the second sides 5 to 8 minutes, again depending on size and your own sense of timing. When they are done, remove them carefully to a hot serving dish, pour the juices over them, and garnish with wedges of lemon. Serves four.

THE SCALIGERI BRIDGE—VERONA   *Veneto Euganea*

Verona Cream of Celery Soup

Crema di Sedani di Verona

(Celery, carrots, leek, butter, egg yolks, cream, Parmesan)

Wash, string, and slice thinly a good head of celery weighing about 2 pounds. Scrape and slice 2 carrots, and clean and slice 1 leek, discarding most of the green part. Heat 4 tablespoons of butter in a deep saucepan, stir the vegetables into this, and cook them slowly for 3 or 4 minutes. Then add 1 cup of hot water and continue cooking the vegetables, covered, until they are soft and well cooked. Force all through a strainer. Return this purée to the stove, and add just enough hot water (about 3 to 4 cups) to give it a good consistency without being too liquid. Season the soup well with salt and pepper, and simmer it again for 5 minutes. Beat together 2 egg yolks, ¾ cup of heavy cream, and 3 tablespoons of grated Parmesan. Blend a little of the soup into this mixture, then add it all gradually to the hot soup, stirring well. Serve at once. Serves six.

CATHEDRAL AT UDINE   *Friuli-Venezia Giulia*

Mixed Salad

Insalata Mista

*(Endive, celery, fennel, potatoes, artichoke hearts, egg, anchovies, parsley,
capers, Swiss cheese, mayonnaise, oil, vinegar)*

Combine in a salad bowl: 1 head of endive, 1 celery heart, and 1 small head
of fennel, all sliced; 2 small boiled potatoes, sliced or diced; 4 artichoke hearts
preserved in oil; and 1 hard-boiled egg, sliced. Add 2 anchovy fillets, cut in pieces,
1 teaspoon of minced parsley, 1 teaspoon of salted Italian capers, rinsed and
dried, and 2 ounces of Swiss cheese cut in julienne strips. Over all pour the
following dressing: To 1 tablespoon of mayonnaise add gradually 1 tablespoon of
wine vinegar, ½ cup of olive oil, and salt and pepper to taste. Mix the salad carefully until the ingredients are well coated. This makes a very good first-course
hors-d'oeuvre or a salad course. Serves four.

THE ALPS, NEAR COURMAYEUR   *Valle d'Aosta*

Stuffed Pheasant

Fagiano Farcito

(Pheasant, butter, bacon, veal, bread crumbs, scallion, parsley, truffle, stock)

In a casserole, melt 1 tablespoon of butter and add 6 or 8 bits of diced bacon. When the fat is hot but not brown, add a cleaned and wiped 3½-pound pheasant. Over moderate heat, brown the bird lightly on all sides. Remove the casserole from the fire, take out the pheasant, and stuff it with the following mixture: Put ¼ pound of lean veal through a meat grinder. Add to the ground meat 3 ounces of diced bacon; the crumbs, without the crust, of 1 slice of stale bread, first soaked in a little stock and squeezed dry; and 1 finely chopped scallion, 1 teaspoon of finely chopped parsley, 1 small diced truffle, and salt and pepper. In place of the truffle you may use 1 or 2 chopped sautéed mushrooms. Truss the bird, tie a slice of bacon over the breast, and return it to the casserole. Put on the lid, and cook the pheasant in a 350° oven for about 1 hour, or until it is tender. For the last 15 minutes of cooking, remove the lid and the strip of bacon. Baste often with the pan juices. At the last, remove some of the fat from the juices, deglaze the pan with a little hot stock, and serve this as a sauce with the pheasant. Serves four.

215

PIAZZA DEL POPOLO FROM THE PINCIO GARDENS *Rome*

Tipsy Cake
Zuppa Inglese

(Sponge cake, rum, raspberry jam, Vanilla Custard, whipped cream, candied fruit)

Slice a 9-inch sponge cake into three layers ½ to ¾ inch thick. Place a layer on a large round serving dish and pour over it ⅓ cup of rum. On it spread about ¾ cup of raspberry jam; strawberry or other preserves may be used if you prefer. Over the jam pour 1½ to 2 cups of Vanilla Custard (*see* Index). Place another slice of cake on this, and spread on it the same amounts of jam and custard. Now place the third slice of cake on top, and pour over it another ⅓ to ½ cup of rum. Let it soak in well, and top the whole with 3 cups of whipped cream flavored with sugar and vanilla (1½ cups of heavy cream before whipping). The top may be decorated with candied fruits. Let the cake stand a while before serving. Serves eight to ten.

216

Menus

❦

LUNCHEONS

Neapolitan salad, 46
Fish with rice in shells, 103
Gorgonzola
Ripe figs or pears

Cucumber and green pepper salad, 78
Veal cutlets Roman style, 37
Buttered noodles, 47
Strawberry ice, 56

❦

❦

Assorted Italian hors-d'oeuvre, 18
Grissini, 190
Fontina cheese mold, 195
Peaches in white wine, 115
Italian almond rusks

Egg salad, 40   Black olives
Italian rice with chicken livers, 49
Green beans sauté, 77
Fontina cheese
Apples

❦

❦

Melon and prosciutto, 44
Crêpes with ricotta, 107
Escarole salad
Marzipan-stuffed apricots, 132
with espresso coffee

Italian meat balls, 133
Purée of potatoes, 88
Tomato salad with basil, 187
Provolone cheese
Fresh grapes

❦

❦

Canned Italian sweet red peppers
with anchovy fillets and lemon
Italian whole-wheat bread
Gnocchi Roman style, 5
Tossed endive, chicory, and
chopped fennel salad
Baked apples in red wine, 48

Caponata, 105
Toasted Italian bread
Poached fish, 124
with green sauce, 28
Steamed new potatoes
Meringues with strawberry whipped-
cream sauce, 29

217

SUPPERS

"Cooked water" soup, 91
Fettuccine with anchovies, 130
Cut-up fruit with Maraschino liqueur

Fish soup with tomatoes, 149
Hot Italian garlic bread
Apricot omelette, 183

❦   ❦

Spaghetti with fresh tomato sauce, 67
Spinach with oil, Genoa style,* 110
Hot wine custard, 41
or cheese and fruit

Rice with egg and lemon, 33
Baked artichokes Sicilian,* 57
Apple fritters, 204
or cheese and fruit

❦   ❦

Chicken consommé, or Italian broth, 76
Grissini, 190
Chicken livers with prosciutto, 95
Boiled rice   Broiled tomatoes
Fresh figs

Sausages in tomato sauce Romagna, 209
Purée of potatoes, 88
Curly chicory salad
Blue cheese
Ripe pears

❦   ❦

Steamed-clam soup, 85
Neapolitan cauliflower salad, 46
Toasted Italian bread
Cream cheese and stewed apricots

Consommé with poached eggs, 24
Stuffed zucchini, 7
Banana fritters, 204
or cheese and fruit

MIDDAY SUNDAY DINNERS

Mixed boiled meats, 136
with green sauce, 28
Boiled potatoes, onions, and cabbage
Tipsy cake, 216
or cheese and fruit

Soave

Ripe honeydew melon, quartered lime
Noodles trasteverina, 160
Asparagus Sunday style,* 202
Assorted cheeses, hot Italian bread
Chocolate ice-cream truffles, 3

Barbera

* Separate course

218

Assorted Italian hors-d'oeuvre, 18
Shin of veal milanese, 179
Italian rice, 116
Sliced bananas and navel oranges
flavored with orange liqueur
Almond macaroons, 66

Chianti

Assorted raw vegetables on ice
Marinated shrimp, 64   Black olives
Green lasagne bolognese, 144
Romaine salad with garlic
Gorgonzola, sweet butter, Italian bread
Biscuit tortoni, 99

Chianti Classico

DINNERS

Buttered noodles, 47
Sea bass in wine sauce, 104
Tossed green salad with garlic croutons
Hot wine custard, 41

Verdicchio di Jesi

Clear soup with custard drops, 158
Chicken breasts Valdostana, 8
Peas with fennel, 182
Frozen chestnut pudding, 63

Barbera

Noodles with pesto, 191
Veal cutlets bolognese, 109
Baked onions in white wine, 120
Assorted Italian cheeses
Ripe persimmons, grapes, shell almonds

Barolo

Salt codfish Vicenza, 185
Boiled potatoes
Baked tomatoes, 69
Assorted Italian cheeses
Dried fruits and nuts

Soave

Grilled shrimp with oil and lemon, 62
Roast chicken bolognese, 113
Browned diced potatoes
Buttered spinach
Stuffed flamed peaches, 13

Barbaresco

Tagliatelle with ham, 74
Cold duck Genoa style, 197
Escarole and chopped fennel salad
Hot baked apples in red wine, 48
Tea cookies, 198

Barolo

Lamb hunter style, 2
Beans Tuscany, 51
Tossed green salad
Assorted Italian cheeses
Banana fritters, 204

Chianti

Shrimp salad antipasto, 98
Florentine beefsteak with lemon, 11
Italian rice with mushrooms, 83
Broiled tomatoes
Apricot soufflé pudding, 192

Chianti Classico

FORMAL DINNER PARTIES

Cocktail Hors-d'Oeuvre:
Hot tomato toast, 169   Marinated shrimp on toothpicks, 64
Italian pickled mushrooms   Imported bite-size grissini

Chicken livornese, 121
Parsleyed steamed potatoes   Fricassee of new carrots, 157
Dry Orvieto

Tossed green salad

Egg-and-butter cream Charlotte, 81
Basket of fresh fruit

Cocktail Hors-d'Oeuvre:
Hot potato sticks, 180   Smoked salmon antipasto on toast, 142
Small black Italian olives

Plain Italian broth, 76, or Roman consommé, 36

Baked fish with green herbs, 112   Verdicchio di Jesi

Beef tenderloin with Madeira, 30   Barolo
Artichokes and peas, 50

Frozen chestnut pudding, 63

Cocktail Hors-d'Oeuvre:
Hot grilled shrimp on toothpicks, 62
Miniature Italian artichoke hearts in oil   Salted pignon nuts

Asparagus mold, 151

Salmi of duck Roman style, 102   Barolo
Italian rice, 116

Tossed endive and chicory salad

Flamed stuffed peaches, 13   Asti Spumante

Cocktail Hors-d'Oeuvre:
Melon balls wrapped in prosciutto, on toothpicks   Italian ripe olives
Creamed Gorgonzola and sweet butter on circles of toast

Trout in white wine, 12   Soave

Roast beef Leghorn, 135   Chianti Classico
Steamed new potatoes   Broccoli Florentine style, 171

Meringues with strawberry whipped-cream sauce, 29

Menu Planner

The bilingual recipe index that follows is designed to serve as a menu planner as well as to locate recipes by name. The English entries, therefore, include the following categories:

Recipe Index

223

226

227

228

231

232